LOWER NEW EN

The Jared Coffin House, Nantucket

COUNTRY INNS OF AMERICA

Lower New England

A GUIDE TO THE INNS OF
CONNECTICUT, MASSACHUSETTS AND RHODE ISLAND

BY PETER ANDREWS, GEORGE ALLEN
AND TRACY ECCLESINE

DESIGNED BY ROBERT REID

HOLT, RINEHART AND WINSTON, *New York*
THE KNAPP PRESS, *Los Angeles*

Frontispiece photograph
Two elegantly-proportioned stained glass windows
filter soft summer light onto the main staircase
at Wheatleigh. Photographed by Lilo Raymond.

Library of Congress Cataloging in Publication Data
Andrews, Peter, 1931–
    Country inns of America.

    Vol. 3 by P. Andrews and T. Ecclesine; vol. 4 by
P. Andrews and G. Allen.
    CONTENTS: [1] Upper New England.—[2] Lower New
England.—[3] New York and Mid-Atlantic.—[4] California.
    1. Hotels, taverns, etc.—California—Directories.
I. Allen, George, 1936–   joint author.
II. Ecclesine, Tracy, joint author. III. Reid, Robert,
1927–   IV. Title.
TX907.A662   647′.94′73   79-22906
ISBN 0 03 043716 4

First Edition

10 9 8 7 6 5 4 3 2 1

A Robert Reid-Wieser & Wieser production

Printed in U.S.A. by R. R. Donnelley & Sons

CONTENTS

Photographed by Lilo Raymond
**Photographed by George W. Gardner*

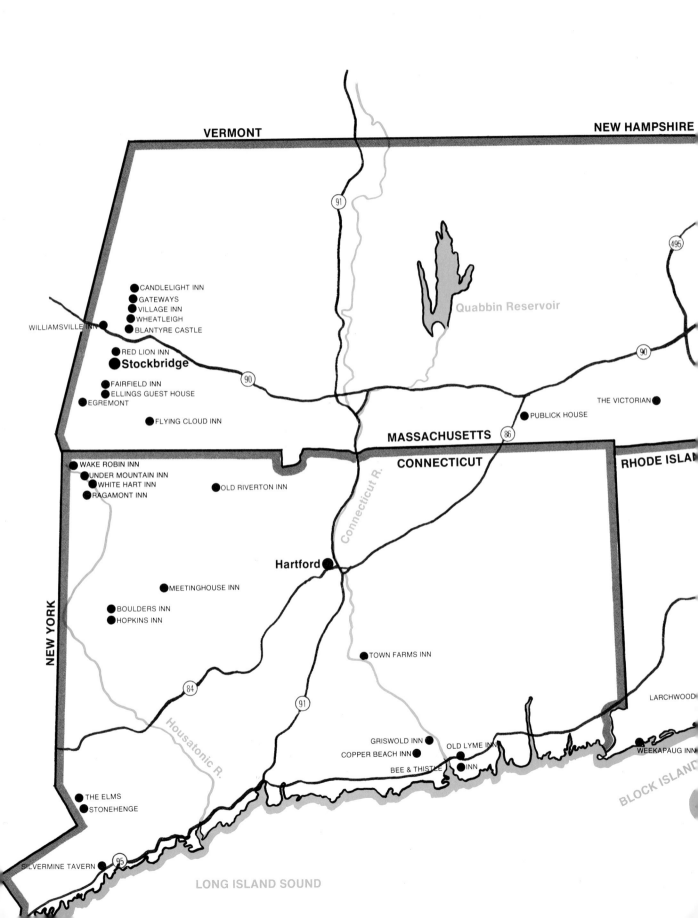

VERMONT

NEW HAMPSHIRE

91

495

Quabbin Reservoir

90

CANDLELIGHT INN
GATEWAYS
VILLAGE INN
WHEATLEIGH
WILLIAMSVILLE INN
BLANTYRE CASTLE

RED LION INN

Stockbridge

90

THE VICTORIAN

FAIRFIELD INN
ELLINGS GUEST HOUSE
EGREMONT

PUBLICK HOUSE

FLYING CLOUD INN

MASSACHUSETTS

86

CONNECTICUT

RHODE ISLAN

WAKE ROBIN INN
UNDER MOUNTAIN INN
WHITE HART INN
RAGAMONT INN

OLD RIVERTON INN

Connecticut R.

NEW YORK

Hartford

MEETINGHOUSE INN

BOULDERS INN
HOPKINS INN

TOWN FARMS INN

LARCHWOOD

84

91

Housatonic R.

GRISWOLD INN
COPPER BEACH INN

OLD LYME INN
INN

BEE & THISTLE

WEEKAPAUG INN

BLOCK ISLAND

THE ELMS
STONEHENGE

SILVERMINE TAVERN

95

LONG ISLAND SOUND

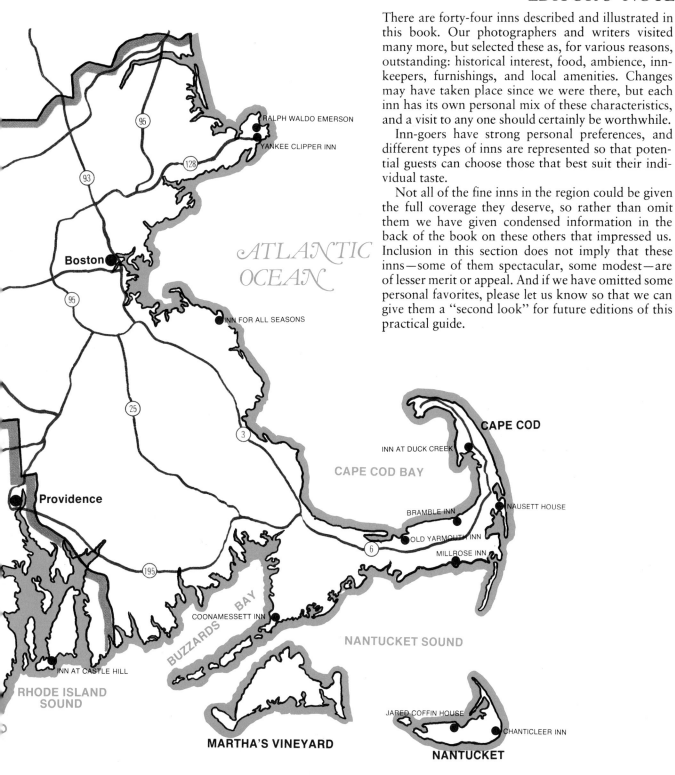

There are forty-four inns described and illustrated in this book. Our photographers and writers visited many more, but selected these as, for various reasons, outstanding: historical interest, food, ambience, innkeepers, furnishings, and local amenities. Changes may have taken place since we were there, but each inn has its own personal mix of these characteristics, and a visit to any one should certainly be worthwhile.

Inn-goers have strong personal preferences, and different types of inns are represented so that potential guests can choose those that best suit their individual taste.

Not all of the fine inns in the region could be given the full coverage they deserve, so rather than omit them we have given condensed information in the back of the book on these others that impressed us. Inclusion in this section does not imply that these inns—some of them spectacular, some modest—are of lesser merit or appeal. And if we have omitted some personal favorites, please let us know so that we can give them a "second look" for future editions of this practical guide.

RALPH WALDO EMERSON
YANKEE CLIPPER INN

ATLANTIC OCEAN

Boston

INN FOR ALL SEASONS

CAPE COD

INN AT DUCK CREEK

CAPE COD BAY

Providence

BRAMBLE INN
NAUSETT HOUSE
OLD YARMOUTH INN
MILLROSE INN

COONAMESSETT INN

BUZZARDS BAY

NANTUCKET SOUND

INN AT CASTLE HILL

RHODE ISLAND SOUND

JARED COFFIN HOUSE
CHANTICLEER INN

MARTHA'S VINEYARD

NANTUCKET

A gracious inn that refreshes the spirit

In a town of great houses, the Bee and Thistle Inn, with its handsome grounds and curving drive, may seem like just one more mansion. But it belongs to Barbara and Gene Bellows, and the relaxation visitors feel immediately on entering the hall is a sign that in Old Lyme, a very traditional town, they have found a most untraditional acceptance and openheartedness.

The house, built late in the eighteenth century, has often been expanded and remodeled, most extensively in the 1920s. The parlors, halls and porches, with their decorative woodwork, consciously reflect the finest in the American tradition. But the inn quickly asserts itself as the comfortable country home it is, full of corners where guests can curl up with a good book.

The food is excellent. Gene Bellows as chief cook whips up shimmering omelettes for breakfast; and for dinner he prepares rich soups and chowders, a fine veal Viennese with a piquant, vinegary touch. Fresh local fish is treated with respect, and dinner concludes with such desserts as yogurt cake and peach Melba.

And then there's the music. Barbara doesn't make a big thing of it, but most evenings she sings folk songs and epic ballads in a sweet voice, accompanying herself on a dulcimer Gene made for her.

At the turn of the century, the ample, aristocratic atmosphere of Old Lyme attracted a whole school of fashionable painters, American Impressionists in love with the varying moods of the landscape and the stately old buildings. Childe Hassam, the most famous, often painted the soaring Old Lyme Meeting House. In the museum next door to the inn, visitors can see these artists' works—paintings of a light-filled world of pleasure among cultured friends.

The Bee and Thistle Inn carries on a genteel cultural tradition that focuses on what novelist William Dean Howells once called "the smiling aspects" of life. To waken in a spacious sunlit room and be served breakfast on a tray, to sit in the small formal garden at the side of the house and write a letter to a friend, to lunch beneath the spreading trees on the front lawn, to spot a seldom-seen variety of bird in the marshes of the Lieutenant River behind the house, to bicycle down the gorgeous main street to the water, where the Connecticut River meets the sea, is to experience gracious living at its best. A visit to the New England shore often brings on a reflective turn of mind and a special spirit of enjoyment not possible elsewhere.

Sun porch restaurant is a delightful addition to the inn.

Indolent mornings at the Bee and Thistle begin with breakfast in bed.

BEE AND THISTLE INN, 100 Lyme St., Old Lyme, Conn. 06371; (203) 434-1667; Gene and Barbara Bellows, Innkeepers. A 10-room inn in a handsome neo-Colonial mansion set in beautiful spacious grounds. Eight rooms with private baths; 2 share bath. The dining room serves breakfast and dinner, and overnight guests may have breakfast in bed. No bar; guests may provide their own wines and liquor. Open all year. Rates $28 to $30 double; single $5 less. Additional person in room $5 more. Children welcome; no pets. Visa credit card accepted. Bicycles available to guests at no charge. Many fine early houses in town; antique, gift, and other exclusive shops. Lyme Art Gallery and Griswold House Historical Museum nearby. Goodspeed Opera House, Essex Steam Train, Mystic Seaport and historic Essex Village a short drive from inn.

DIRECTIONS: Train from Boston or New York City stops at Old Saybrook station. By car from New York City, take I-95 North to Exit 70. Exit left off ramp. From Boston or Providence, take I-95 South to Exit 70. Right off ramp.

Feasting with flair in a country inn

Architect Mies van der Rohe once said, "God is in the details." Van der Rohe worked with steel and glass. Jo and Bob McKenzie work with crystal, silver, cut flowers, the best and freshest of foods and a dedicated and skilled staff. God is surely in the details at the Copper Beech Inn, a hostelry where even a short visit is a celebration of good living.

The inn occupies a sprawling mansion set on a rise behind a wide-spreading copper beech tree, possibly the oldest in Connecticut. To judge from the interiors, the ivory merchant who once lived here had a princely concept of life. When the McKenzies restored the house six years ago, they kept the spacious bedrooms and baths intact, and Jo decorated them with an inspired ensemble of wallpapers, wicker furniture, bright comforters and antiques that sets off the palatial character of the house to perfection.

The foyer and dining rooms have an atmosphere of restrained elegance. Queen Anne armchairs are drawn up at widely spaced tables in the Ivoryton Room. From each crystal wineglass emerges the double taper of a rolled linen napkin. Brass chandeliers light the large room, and brass lamps gleam on the blue-papered walls. In the paneled Comstock Room, the central mahogany dining table is never covered with a cloth; its rich surface gleams brightly beneath table settings of the finest silver and china.

The Copper Beech Inn often has an atmosphere of anticipation that is seldom sensed in a restaurant but often in a theater. Diners seem to regard each new course as a development in a drama. Abetting this feeling, the accomplished waiters never miss a line or a cue. They serve every dish with a flourish, and each meal proceeds full of striking incident and gracious motion. The body is nourished, but so are the spirit and the imagination.

To start, try twin baby trout in a mustard sauce, hot country pâté with truffle sauce, quenelles of salmon or poached mussels Niçoise. Soups include the inn's famous lobster bisque, but chef Ray Terrill always presents his current enthusiasm, as well. Many entrées are sautéed—trout meunière, sweetbreads with mustard butter, frogs legs Provençale. Rarely are dishes heavily sauced—roast duckling with sauce Périgourdine is an exception.

The pride, care, imagination and skill that go into a day's hospitality at the Copper Beech Inn are so enormous that visitors feel it would be easier to stage grand opera every day than to consistently produce such magnificent food and service.

Flowered wallpaper and wicker chairs reflect a summery mood.

A garden within a garden: the old greenhouse is now a cool, elegant piano bar filled with ferns, flowers and Chinese Chippendale.

THE COPPER BEECH INN, Main St., Ivoryton, Conn. 06442; (203) 767-0330; Robert and Jo McKenzie, Innkeepers. A 5-room inn celebrated for the only 4-star restaurant in Connecticut. Serving lunch and dinner, the restaurant specializes in Country French cuisine and unusually attentive service. Open all year except Mondays and Christmas. Rates $42.80 single or double. Children under 3 not encouraged. No pets. Visa, Master Charge, American Express and Diners Club credit cards accepted. Summer theater in town; boating, tennis and antiquing nearby.

DIRECTIONS: From New York City, take I-95 North to Exit 69, which will lead into Conn. Route 9. Take Exit 3, left 1½ miles to inn.

As comfortable and familiar as a club

Ridgefield is one of the closest towns to New York City with the look and feel of a New England village. All the elements are there, including ancient houses and fine old churches, reminders of a time when private property and public pride went hand in hand.

The buildings of The Elms Inn stand on ample grounds across from a town park. Built in the 1760s, the house became an inn in 1799. When more room was needed, early owners added on to the back. With its red carriage barn, shingled water tower from the 1880s and big frame Victorian annex, the inn today reflects its long and continuous growth.

To local residents, The Elms Inn is as comfortable and familiar as a club, and visitors from the city retreat here to country pleasures. While the prize guest rooms are those made from the old ballroom upstairs, with their vaulted ceilings and fireplaces, all the rooms have the settled charm of an old, well-cared-for home. The Elms Inn is the pride of innkeeper Robert Scala and his family, and the family of his brother, the late Mario Scala, who developed the menu and long served as chef de cuisine.

Off the wide central hall, in the brightly decorated dining rooms, domestic in scale, a meal is an opportunity to share a joyful visit with friends. In the taproom, with its bare floors and no-nonsense tavern chairs, the casual, cheerful atmosphere sparks genial talk.

The wide-ranging menu includes tournedos Helder, rack of lamb, poached salmon with hollandaise and veal Venus, tender scallops of veal covered with a mousse of mushrooms and a little hollandaise that are slipped for a moment under the broiler and then served with Madeira sauce. There is gravelax, a marvelous Norwegian salmon appetizer, and zabaglione, a favorite Italian dessert. Quail is available in season, and The Elms Inn uses the best occasions to hold a celebration: a morel party to herald a new shipment of the marvelous mushrooms; and a January sanglier, a traditional feast of wild boar for the turn of the year, which may also include filet of sole Dieppoise and a gâteau St. Honoré. A proper selection of wines is al-

Once a ballroom, now a guest room.

ways available; Bobby Scala is proud of his extensive and carefully stocked cellar.

Time is catching up with Ridgefield, even at The Elms; the annex will soon be remodeled into suites to dazzle and refresh the traveler. As long as there is a Scala to extend the hand of hospitality, though, the warm spirit of the old inn will never lapse. They're just getting it ready for its third century.

THE ELMS, 163 Main St., Ridgefield, Conn. 06877; (203) 438-2541; Robert Scala, Innkeeper. A 10-room Colonial-style inn dating from 1799, renowned for superlative dining. Private baths in all but one room. Open all year. Complete breakfast available to overnight guests. The famed restaurant serves lunch and dinner featuring Continental cuisine. The extensive cellar specializes in the finest French and American wines. Rates $35 double, $25 single. Children welcome; no pets. Visa, Master Charge, American Express and Diners Club credit cards accepted. Public golf course and swimming nearby.

DIRECTIONS: From New York City, take Sawmill River Pkwy. Turn off east on Route 35, which becomes Main Street when it enters Ridgefield. Inn is catercorner to Ballard Park.

A pre-revolutionary house built by a cabinet maker.

A marine masterpiece on a charming waterfront

William Winterer is a sailor who loves boats and the sea. So naturally he lives in Essex, which has been a sailor's haven for more than 200 years. He discovered Essex in 1957, when he was a cadet at the Coast Guard Academy in New London, but there was another attraction besides the historic town.

"I was in love with the old Griswold," he recalls. "The Tap Room was the handsomest bar I had ever seen in America. Besides being a wonderful tavern, the Griswold had one of the finest collections of marine art in the nation, and I fell under its spell. I had a fifteen-year courtship with the Griswold, and in 1972 I consummated it by giving up my career as an investment banker and buying the place to become an innkeeper."

The inn was the very first three-story house built in Connecticut, and except for the removal of a second-floor gallery, it has remained virtually unchanged for 200 years. The Tap Room has a huge potbellied stove, which is kept burning from autumn until early spring, and an antique popcorn machine, which is still serving it up, hot and buttered. The original parlor is now a book-lined dining room, and the Steamboat Room is fitted out to duplicate the dining room of one of the

old steamers that once plied its way between Hartford and New York City. The fabulous art collection and other marine memorabilia are dispersed throughout the richly paneled downstairs rooms.

Winterer explains his philosophy on innkeeping: "Our rooms are centuries away from motel accommodations. Our brass beds and noninsistence on having a private bath in every room bear witness to that. Some of the floors upstairs have a port or starboard list that is over a century old, too, but that's the way we like the Griswold to be."

In keeping with its venerable status, the Griswold plays an important part in the civic and social life of the town. Lunch at the inn is an institution, and some of the tables are permanently reserved for the regulars. Another custom is the English hunt breakfast, started by the British during their occupation of Essex in the War of 1812 and still held every Sunday morning.

Winterer says: "You know, in Colonial times the local innkeeper was one of the most important men. His inn was an informal meeting place for everyone to meet and talk over their problems. The tradition of the American innkeeper is a valuable one, and we are trying to maintain it."

Pleasure craft crowd the marina.

Visitors love the absence of telephones in guest rooms. OVERLEAF: pictures from the inn's fabled collection of marine art line the walls and sloping ceilings of The Tap Room.

GRISWOLD INN, Main St., Essex, Conn. 06426; (203) 767-0991; William and Victoria Winterer, Innkeepers. This 20-room inn occupies a 200-year-old building that is virtually unchanged. Private baths, air conditioning. Rates $32 to $40, single or double, with Continental breakfast. Open all year except Christmas. Large dining room serves lunch and dinner daily. Special menus for children. Popular Hunt Breakfast Sunday noon to 2:30 P.M. Pets accepted. Visa, Master Charge and American Express credit cards accepted. Sailing. Nostalgic Tap Room; fabulous collection of art and marine memorabilia in public rooms.

DIRECTIONS: From New York City, take I-95 to Conn. Route 9. Take Essex Exit 3 onto Route 153, which becomes Main St. Inn in town center.

ON SERVED ONLY

12 - 1 30 ᴘᴍ

Monday

CLO

SER

WEE

SATUR

SUNDA

Dinner

Appetizers: Tomato or Grapefruit Juice .50
Pate Maison 1.00 Egg à la Jacques 1.00 Baby Trout 1.75
Herring 1.25 Shrimp Cocktail all 2.50 Escargot 2.75
Clams Casino 2.75 Hearts of Palm 1.25 Bundnerfeller ns
Pepper + Anchovies 1.25 Spinach Salad 1.50 Gazpacho 1.00
Melon + Prosciutto 1.75 Soup du Jour

Filet of Sole Almandine — — — — — 8.25
Broiled Salmon — — — — — 9.25
Soft Shell Crabs — — — — — 9.25
Chicken Cordon Bleu — — — — 7.75
Broiled Sirloin steak — — — — — 10.50
Wienerschnitzel — — — — — 8.75
Calves Brains au Beurre Noir — — — 7.75
Loin Lamb Chops — — — — — 9.25
Broiled Sweetbreads — — — — 9.25
Roast Duck à l'orange — — — — 8.15
Piccata Milanaise — — — — — 8.75
Sea Scallops in Garlic Butter — — — 9.25
Hungarian Goulash — — — — 8.75
Backhendl — — — — — 7.75
Prime Rib of Beef — — — — 9.75

Austrian flair on a Connecticut lake

The country around Lake Waramaug has the look of long cultivation and use, but it hasn't been overrun by houses or bathing beaches. There are splendid views of the lake from the porches of the Hopkins Inn and from the large stone terrace at its side, as well as from several of its old-fashioned guest rooms, with their floral wallpapers, smoky mirrors, wicker chairs and white-painted woodwork. The view isn't the sole reason for the inn's popularity, however. Guests come primarily to dine.

Innkeeper Franz Schober is Austrian; chef Seppi Mueller is Swiss. Theirs is a cuisine without a hint of excess, except perhaps in the texture of such dishes as calves brains au beurre noir. The spicing of the Wiener schnitzel and the roast pork paprika is handled with European discretion. The offerings are seasonal—poached salmon in summer, plentiful game in fall. Among the beautifully presented appetizers is a light liver pâté with a distinctive flavor. Prosciutto and melon make a wonderful start for a summer luncheon, which might continue with spinach salad or chicken Cordon Bleu. The Hopkins Inn pulls out all the stops with its rich desserts—a smooth white-chocolate mousse, meringue glacé and a variety of sundaes.

The day's dishes are announced on a slate brought to the table by a smiling waitress in dirndl skirt and peasant blouse. In warm weather, luncheon and dinner are served on the terrace. Indoors, there are two delightful dining rooms. One, with a view of the lake, has fanciful Austrian chandeliers and chairs in the Early American style. The other is darkly paneled and has the feel of a Gasthaus. Its marvelous fireplace is faced with figured tiles depicting the story of Rip Van Winkle in vibrant, earthy colors.

A foyer leads to the inn's bar, in the oldest portion of the building, an eighteenth-century farmhouse. The main part of the inn is a blocky, ample Greek Revival house with cupola, built in the 1840s by George C. Hopkins. The décor of its parlors still echoes the taste of the Victorian era, with curved sofas, overstuffed chairs, marble-topped tables and floral prints. After dinner, little more is needed to complete the evening than a stroll around the porch and grounds. Then to bed, drifting off to sleep to the sound of leaves rustling gently in the maples and the water lapping the shore of the lake below.

Early American décor contrasts with Austrian Room's splendor beyond.

Tyrolean treat: waitresses in Austrian dirndles lend a colorful air to dining at Hopkins Inn. OVERLEAF: terrace lunch at the Hopkins is a local tradition.

THE HOPKINS INN, New Preston, Conn. 06777; (203) 868-7295; Franz and Beth Schober, Innkeepers. A comfortable, homelike, 10-room inn on Lake Waramaug; 7 rooms with private baths, 3 rooms share baths. Open from May through Oct. A 2-room suite with kitchenette, available from Easter to New Year, accommodates 3. The restaurant, open Tuesday through Sunday, April to Jan., seats 90, or guests may dine on the terrace. A complete breakfast is served and dinner is selected from an extensive Continental menu. Attractive Tavern room. Rates are $22 to $25, double, with private baths; $16 to $20 double, with shared baths. Suite $32. Single occupancy, $2 less. Children welcome; no pets. No credit cards accepted. Private beach on lake.

DIRECTIONS: From New York City, take Sawmill River Pkwy. to Route 684. Follow to I-84 East, to 7 and 202 North. Take 202 to New Preston. Turn left on Route 45 past Lake Waramaug. Take first left and second right to inn.

Treasure-trove inn in Connecticut

The Silvermine Tavern was originally built as a saw-mill more than 200 years ago. It became an inn almost by accident. Bought in the 1920s by Ken Byard, a well-known New York antiques and art dealer, it was made over into a store and art gallery. Since New York City was quite a hike in those days, he invited his friends to stay over in the nearby guest house. When some of his old customers asked if they could spend a night or two, he gradually found himself running a full-fledged tavern and country inn.

Today the tavern is part of a complex of buildings, run by Francis Whitman, Jr., and his father, with additional accommodations in the Coach House and Old Mill. Most of the décor and art objects throughout the tavern are from Byard's collections. The guest rooms are Colonial in style, many with canopied beds. A major attraction is the Country Store, just across the street, which is both an emporium and an informal museum. It is a splendid evocation of the days when everybody in town stopped by the general store to do their shopping and catch up on the news. Today, the store sells New England food specialties and old-fashioned candy, along with Early American reproductions. The checkerboard, set up right next to the mandatory potbellied stove, is always at the ready. At the heart of the complex is the tavern itself, which, under the Whitman family's direction, has become a major restaurant in the area. The main dining room is highlighted by a large brick fireplace painted white and many eighteenth-century artifacts, including "Miss Abigail," a re-creation of a Colonial lady in a poke bonnet, long dress and shawl, who is the only woman allowed by Connecticut state law to stand within three feet of the bar. In good weather, dining on the tavern's large, sun-dappled wooden deck overlooking the millpond, with its two dazzling white swans, is an unforgettable experience.

Just down the road from the tavern is one of the most unusual community associations in America, the Silvermine Guild of Artists, a combination of studios, workshops, galleries and schools, where all

The only woman allowed to stand at a bar in Connecticut.

the arts—painting, sculpture, music and dance—are pursued in an atmosphere of mutual cooperation. It is well worth a visit.

Silvermine got its name in the eighteenth century, when an early settler claimed to have found a silver mine at nearby Comstock Hills. The rumor was soon found to be false, but more than 200 years later, the Silvermine Tavern is the genuine article, a real treasure.

SILVERMINE TAVERN, corner of Perry and Silvermine Aves., Norwalk, Conn. 06850; (203) 847-4558; Francis Whitman, Sr. and Francis Whitman, Jr., Innkeepers. A 10-room inn in a bucolic far suburb of New York City. Private baths. Open all year. Rates $32 to $35 double; $20 to $22 single, including Continental breakfast. Lunch and dinner served daily. Children welcome; pets accepted at discretion of innkeepers. Visa, Master Charge, American Express and Diners Club credit cards accepted. Authentic country store across the street, Silvermine Artists Guild nearby.

DIRECTIONS: From New York City, take Merritt Parkway to Exit 39; turn onto Route 7 South. At first traffic light turn right on Perry Ave., which winds 2½ miles to tavern.

Tall, stately trees shade the outdoor dining deck at Silvermine. OVERLEAF: a treasure-trove of toys and tools from a bygone era adorn the inn.

Haute cuisine in a bucolic setting

Stonehenge matches haute cuisine with a Connecticut Colonial setting out of a Peter De Vries novel. Ducks, swans and Canada geese swim in a wide, tree-bordered pond, and low-lying cottages form a complex around an old farmhouse with a pine-paneled pleasure dome of a dining room where all the best traditions of fine dining are upheld.

The tables are set with superb china and candles hooded with red parchment shades. In the bar, there are enough old prints and dark corners to make even the most urban diner feel like a country squire just in from the hunt. A window in the wall provides a view of the wine cellar, housing a collection of extraordinary vintages.

Crêpes, stuffed with mushrooms and Gruyère cheese, in a Mornay sauce, or the shrimp in beer batter with a pungent fruit sauce are a wonderful way to start a meal. Most spectacular of the entrées is the brook trout "en bleu," in which the fish are kept alive in a tank and poached at the last minute in a court bouillon laced with vinegar, which turns the fish blue. They are then skinned and boned at the table and served with a mousseline sauce; Stonehenge is justly famous for this dish. Other choices include breast of capon with white grapes in a cream sauce; Long Island duckling with pears and lingonberries, flambé; and filet of beef Wellington, with a truffled sauce Périgourdine. Salads are mixed at the table by a solemn

Angled walls and fireplace in guest room are reminders that Stonehenge was once a farmhouse.

waiter, and in fact the serious and deliberate service makes it quite clear that fine dining is indeed one of the sacred rituals of civilization.

Desserts match the extraordinary heights of the earlier courses. A vanilla custard topped with a cake crust is both light and rich, even without its delicious strawberry sauce. The flavor of the dark chocolate cake is so profound diners' eyes cloud over, and the mocha tart, with a crust of ground walnuts, calls a halt to conversation for at least ten minutes.

The perfect place for a romantic meal, Stonehenge also offers a more than ordinary overnight stay. The guest rooms are spacious and studded with antiques. In the morning, Continental breakfast is served in the room—juice, good strong coffee and one of the inn's perfect pastries.

Stonehenge opened in 1948 and was one of the first establishments of its kind to be compared favorably with the best in Europe. The founder, owner and chef de cuisine was the late, legendary Albert Stockli, who ran it for two decades. Today, Stonehenge continues in the fine tradition that he established.

The library and sitting room.

A verdant and cooling oasis: the man-made falls and pond at Stonehenge. OVERLEAF: the inn, with its mill pond migrants.

STONEHENGE, P.O. Box 667, Route 7, Danbury-Norwalk Rd., Ridgefield, Conn. 06877; (203) 438-6511; David Davis and Douglas Seville, Innkeepers. An early 19th-century Colonial-style inn with 2 rooms and 6 cottages. Private baths, air conditioning, black and white TV. Lunch and dinner featuring Continental cuisine served in 3 dining rooms overlooking duck pond. Continental breakfast served in rooms for overnight guests. Open all year except Tuesdays. Rates $35 and $45 double. Cots available for third person in larger rooms. Children welcome; no pets. Visa, Master Charge, American Express and Diners Club credit cards accepted. Swimming pool.

DIRECTIONS: From New York City, take Merritt Pkwy. to Exit 40 onto Route 7, North. Inn is 13 miles north on left-hand side.

From poorhouse to country inn

There's a great deal of high living going on at the poorhouse these days. Town Farms Inn was once Middletown's poor farm, but Bill and Vicky Winterer recently bought the old brick farmstead and transformed it into a festive new country inn.

The beautifully paneled lobby is impeccably furnished with Colonial-style chairs and sofas and nineteenth-century primitive paintings. Staffordshire dogs rest on the fireplace mantel. Flowers, some freshly cut and others of delicate silk, are arranged in luxuriant displays throughout the rooms. "No expense has been spared," says Sal Carta, the maître d'.

The American Indian room, with its rich red walls, beamed ceilings, round tables and wide, comfortable Windsor armchairs, is a perfect replica of a comfortable private club. In the high hall of the River Room, hung with two vast and beautiful pressed-glass chandeliers, the Winterers have evoked a bit of each era from New England's past and added some European touches. A Palladian window sheds light on pale blue neo-Georgian woodwork. There is a musicians' gallery reminiscent of Restoration England, and a panoramic mural depicts the Connecticut River in the nineteenth century, alive with sailing craft and steamboats. Tall French doors open onto a terrace that looks out on the river itself, just across the road.

The sitting room: Early American warmth.

Opening off the River Room is a tiny private dining area decorated like the inside of a tent. There is also a marvelous dining room where the walls have been stripped down to the brick and hung with photographs of Middletown in earlier days. The lodgings to be added in 1979 will complete what is already one of the most fetching social environments in New England.

Bill Winterer, also owner and manager of the Griswold Inn in Essex, has made sure that the food and service match the décor in quality and imagination. The varied menu features hare in wine, impressive veal dishes and well-prepared fish. Town Farms's bouillabaisse is a French classic with a local Yankee accent, as are the mussels in cream sauce.

The starched crispness of the linen, the single rose on each table, the young and enthusiastic staff, the spirit of infectious good humor—all have combined to create a classic country inn in only two years. Sometimes, when the ingredients are just right, it can happen that quickly.

The American Indian dining room.

Town Farms's bold, red brick exterior houses some fine treasures. The glowing chandeliers in the River Room, *left*, were purchased in Europe by the inn's owners, who later discovered that the antique fixtures were the work of Connecticut Valley craftsmen.

TOWN FARMS INN, River Rd. at Silver St., Middletown, Conn. 06457; (203) 347-7438; William and Victoria Winterer, Innkeepers. A 12-room inn in an elegant country house on the Connecticut River, carefully restored and luxuriously decorated. Private baths. The dining room specializes in Country Continental cuisine at lunch and dinner. Special menu for children. Hunt Breakfast, Sunday from noon to 2:30, is popular. Open all year except Christmas. Write or phone for rates and reservations. Pets accepted. Visa, Master Charge and American Express credit cards accepted. Boating, sailing.

DIRECTIONS: From New York City, take Hutchinson River Pkwy., Route 684 to Route 84. Turn right and drive through Danbury and Waterbury to Route 66. Continue to Middletown and watch for inn signs.

A "revolutionary" hostelry

An ancient honey locust tree spreads its crown above Under Mountain Inn's roof, and mature birches and maples arch over the long, elliptical yard. The building is venerable, a 1732 Colonial farmstead grown into a generous, many-gabled structure, with a flagstone patio at the side and a wide front porch. Inside the broad front door, a central hall, a little out of plumb, confirms both the age and durability of the house. Beyond is a warren of intimate dining rooms with fireplaces, warmed as much by the patina of centuries-old paneling and furnishings as by the cheerfully burning logs. New England travelers have long gathered around candlelit tables in houses like this to partake of an innkeeper's goodly fare. At the Under Mountain Inn, Continental taste has altered native ways a bit, because chalked on the menu slate are a range of dishes such as escargots in mushroom caps, salmon in champagne sauce and sweetbreads with capers in sherry sauce, along with the usual prime ribs of beef. The breakfasts add an unusual warm zucchini bread to the traditionally American eggs and bacon. The inn also serves a popular weekend brunch.

The taproom is paneled with wood found in the house, fruit of an instance of Colonial defiance. So precious was the wood of New England to the English king that any tree as large as twenty-four inches in diameter was designated "The King's Wood," to be

Pewterware gleams on the dining room tables.

used for masts on British sailing vessels. Not all the big ones got away, though, because the taproom's walls are completely covered with boards twenty-four inches wide, trophies of rebellion, proudly shown.

Decoration throughout the inn hints at the revolutionary, too, with an eagle motif on the wallpaper and the figures of militiamen on the patterned pillow covers and prints. But no rebellion is likely against the braided rugs and comfortable wing chairs of the guest rooms. One vast, luxurious bath contains a marvelous claw-footed cast-iron tub raised on a platform.

There may be an Italian racing magazine or two in the guest rooms, since drivers and aficionados frequent the inn during the auto races at nearby Lime Rock. Tanglewood is close, and chamber music may be heard at Music Mountain. Beyond the wide upland meadows behind the inn, the ridge of the Taconic Mountains rises; horses graze in fields nearby—a perfect setting for the civilized and civilizing influence of the Under Mountain Inn.

UNDER MOUNTAIN INN, Undermountain Rd. (Route 41), Salisbury, Conn. 06068; (203) 435-0242; Al and Lorraine Bard, Innkeepers. A 7-room inn in an Early American farmhouse in the shadow of the Taconic Mountains. Private baths. Open all year except Mondays and Tuesdays, and for 3 weeks in early spring. Rates, including Continental breakfast, $38.50 and $43.50 double or single. Children welcome; no pets. No credit cards accepted. Four dining rooms, including popular Colonial taproom, serve a complete breakfast, dinner featuring American and Continental cuisine, and Saturday and Sunday brunch. Twin Lakes within walking distance for swimming, sailing, canoeing. Tennis and golf available nearby. Auto racing in season at Lime Rock; music at Tanglewood and Music Mountain.

DIRECTIONS: From New York City, take Major Deegan to N.Y. Thruway to Route 287 East to Route 684 North to Route 22 North to Route 343 East to Route 41 North. Inn is on Route 41, 4 miles north of center of town of Salisbury.

The guest rooms are delightful.

Mountain laurel flourishes in the wooded countryside around the inn, left above; a white picket fence camouflages the bar. OVERLEAF: once a private club, Under Mountain Inn stands surrounded by fine, old trees.

Art and artistry on Cape Cod

Some country inns are live-in museums. The Bramble Inn is a live-in art gallery, and every step of the way there's something new to catch the eye.

There are six rooms and three guest rooms in this century-old white Cape Cod house, and all have been carefully arranged to show off the innkeepers' collection of quality contemporary art.

The inn/art gallery is the brainchild of Elaine Brennan and Karen Etsell, who bought it four years ago after longtime careers as psychiatric social workers. They both grew up in the Northeast and have long loved Cape Cod. For them, the inn is a kind of political statement—it is another way to provide service, to be independent and to overcome the mediocrity of public institutions.

Every detail at the Bramble Inn is thoughtfully integrated into an overall scheme, resulting in a delightfully rich dining experience and a comfortable sojourn upstairs. The food selection is limited, but delectable: an assortment of cheese plates, crêpes and desserts, among them the Cape Cod Bramble à la mode—an old-fashioned delicacy of chopped raisins and cranberries, egg whites and what Karen guardedly calls

"secrets" wrapped in a tender pastry and served with a scoop of ice cream.

The quiche, an eye-catching patchwork of yellows and browns, served with a fresh green salad, also has a secret ingredient that is almost indiscernible. The innkeepers describe the quiche as "haughty, pungent and satiating," and it more than lives up to its advance billing.

The color scheme of the dining rooms, adapted from the Polo Lounge in Beverly Hills, is a bold pink and green that is repeated down to the last detail, even to the hand-painted enamel napkin rings. Linking the three sunny dining rooms in an almost continuous pattern is a potpourri of artistic media—collotype prints, wood-lathe art, hand-formed paper, etchings, rubbings, photographs (many by Elaine), *oshibana*—pressed flowers on rice paper—and several works by prominent West Coast artist Jacqueline Draeger.

Located on the main road in the quiet town of Brewster, the inn is within walking distance of the ocean and is adjacent to tennis courts and nearby to golf, fishing, museums, a state park, a summer theater and many other Cape Cod resort and recreational activities.

Guest rooms are another spot for the contemporary art collection.

The dining room doubles as a contemporary art gallery, and the gift shop features treats for the palate as well as the eye.

BRAMBLE INN, Route 6A, P.O. Box 159, Brewster, Mass. 02631; (617) 896-7644; Elaine Brennan and Karen Etsell, Innkeepers. A 3-room Cape Cod house that doubles as a stunning art gallery. Shared baths; TV in each room. Open from late May through October. Closed Mondays. Rates $22.50 off season; $28.50 in season, single or double, with complimentary Continental breakfast. Lunch and dinner are served in three cheerful dining rooms. No children overnight; no pets. No credit cards accepted. Tennis courts nearby. Dennis Playhouse and Orleans Academy Playhouse 5 miles from inn.

DIRECTIONS: From Route 6, Mid-Cape Highway, take Exit 10 North to Route 6A. After 4 miles, turn right. Inn is 1/10-mile on left.

Gourmet delights on Nantucket

Nantucket is an island of contrasts. At one end is "the town," a bustling tourist mecca for summer day-trippers, and at the other side of the island is "S'conset" (a contraction of Siasconset), a sleepy little outpost that approaches the end of the world.

S'conset is a storybook collection of weathered gray houses, a tiny post office, a market, coffee shop and little else—except for that glittering oasis of French cuisine, The Chanticleer Inn. A favorite among local summer residents, The Chanticleer Inn is fast becoming renowned, and many out-of-towners spend their annual "food holiday" at the inn.

Jean Berruet, the young French owner, has come a long way since his early childhood in Brittany. After writing to Earle MacAusland, a Nantucket resident and publisher of *Gourmet* magazine, about the possibility of jobs for a French chef who liked to travel, he was hired as MacAusland's personal chef, a position he held for several years. Berruet then moved on to become chef at The Chanticleer, and from there it was a small step to becoming the owner.

The inn's most popular dishes, the Coquilles St. Jacques poached in Madeira sauce with truffles and served on spinach, and the scallopini of bass sautéed with shallots, dry vermouth, heavy cream and sorrel, speak for themselves. To add a bit of exotica, The Chanticleer Inn features roast quail in a brandy sauce with fresh grapes, smoked eels (which Berruet smokes in his backyard) in a yogurt sauce with herbs, and a rabbit pâté with juniper berries. Local products are played up—Nantucket Bay scallops, bluefish, which is smoked, and crab, used in crab soup. The wine list is extensive.

Reservations for lunch or dinner must be made several days in advance in the summer.

During the day, guests might want to bicycle to the town of Nantucket, seven miles away, and gaze at the old sea captains' mansions or explore the shops and beaches. But for local sightseeing, nothing beats the S'conset weather vanes. Starkly realistic, the menagerie that crowns the silver-shingled houses includes fish, horses and cows. Back in the inn's courtyard is the reigning member of the animal family—a gaily

Chef-owner Jean Berruet in the most famous courtyard in S'conset.

Elegance of cuisine is matched by dining décor.

painted wooden horse that is probably the most photographed item in S'conset. Tourists are constantly jumping out of cars or buses to pose for just one snapshot.

Cottage rooms at The Chanticleer Inn are modest but comfortable, tucked away behind rose-covered trellises. The hot-water supply may be somewhat erratic, but this seems a small price to pay to enjoy so many treasures for the eye and palate.

THE CHANTICLEER INN, Siasconset, Nantucket, Mass. 02564; (617) 257-6231; Jean Charles Berruet, Innkeeper. Renowned for its superlative French cuisine, this island inn has 6 cottage guest rooms with private baths. Children and pets accepted. Open from about May 20 to Columbus Day. Rates from about $32 off season to about $40 in season, double. Complimentary Continental breakfast for inn guests. Restaurant serves lunch and dinner and advance reservations are imperative. American Express credit card accepted. Ocean beaches; old mansions and shops in town of Nantucket.

DIRECTIONS: From ferry dock at Nantucket, go up Main St. to Orange St., then to S'conset Rd. Continue 8 miles and make a right on New St.

Working fireplaces and homemade bread

At first glance, the three-story Egremont Inn may seem a bit overpowering, but once you cross the threshold you'll probably feel right at home. Innkeepers Rudyard Propst, a psychologist, and his wife, Robin, a fund raiser, will welcome you warmly to their cozy abode.

The inn has been sheltering tired travelers since 1780, when it was Hare's Tavern, a stagecoach stop on the Albany–Hartford run. The Propsts have been at the inn a little over a year, and Rudyard confesses to having had inn fantasies for a long time. His desire: to run an attractive place where people could feel comfortable, make new friends and feel a part of something. The inn has a family feeling, according to Rudyard, and, indeed, many of the staff are related to each other and live almost around the corner.

The Egremont is primarily a weekend place. In summer, there are Tanglewood, summer theater, museums, antique and crafts shops, riding and golf. And there's always time out in between for a set of tennis on one of the inn's two courts or swimming in the pool. Guests may also refresh themselves on the large front porch, where lunch and dinner are served, usually to a sell-out crowd. The porch overlooks a small brook and two huge sycamores, which are said to date back to 1812.

In winter, guests congregate around many comfortable sitting areas and five working fireplaces, warming up for a day on the slopes or out on the prowl through picturesque New England towns. The inn serves what it calls its "light menu" at all times, in addition to full-course meals. The open-face sandwiches on homemade bread continue to be popular favorites, especially the shrimp and avocado, roast beef with tuna mayonnaise and organic peanut butter with chutney.

For dinner, veal dishes are well liked as is the fresh fish. The chicken breasts Alba are a pleasant blend of chicken, mushrooms and fontina cheese. Sunday brunch is gaining a following, and the seafood strudel, made with phyllo dough, seafood, onions, chopped eggs and hollandaise sauce, is especially popular. For special buffets and parties, Robin has developed meatless dishes—an eggplant curry, and feta cheese and spinach pie.

A corner in the main sitting room.

As for guest rooms, the inn has 23 comfortable rooms with private baths and one suite. Rooms vary in size and are old-fashioned, clean and comfortable. Some have desks, others have antique chests and secretaries, and there is even a brass bed or two. The Egremont has no televisions or telephones, because, as the innkeepers are fond of pointing out, they didn't think old Mr. Hare, the founder, would have wanted them.

THE EGREMONT INN, Old Sheffield Rd., South Egremont, Mass. 01258; (413) 528-2111; Rudyard and Robin Propst, Innkeepers. This 23-room inn is a popular weekend retreat. Private baths and air conditioning. Open all year, except from mid-March to mid-April and from Oct. 31 to Thanksgiving. Rates $35 to $48, double, weekends, $28 to $38 double, midweek. Dining room open daily for lunch and dinner, except Mondays. Sunday brunch. Children welcome, no pets. Visa and Master Charge. Swimming pool, tennis courts. Riding, golf, summer theater. Tanglewood Music Festival, antique and craft shops all nearby.

DIRECTIONS: From New York City, take Taconic Pkwy. to Route 23 East. Continue 14 miles to South Egremont. Old Sheffield Rd. is off Route 23; look for sign.

Back to nature
in the Berkshires

Take a 1771 converted farmhouse in an idyllic setting, complete with its own natural pond and 200 acres of backwoods, add a charming young couple as hosts, set them all down in the middle of the Berkshires, serve simply prepared homegrown foods and we have the Flying Cloud Inn.

Located twenty-five minutes from Tanglewood, the Flying Cloud Inn, named after a famous nineteenth-century clipper ship, is a favorite among music lovers as well as antique buffs, tennis players and cross-country skiers.

The inn has its own live-in tennis pro in summer, which is pretty plush for just two courts. The Flying Cloud Inn is one of those establishments where guests may either do nothing or almost everything, including kayaking and rowing on the spring-fed pond, ice skating, bicycling, or playing baseball, croquet, badminton, volleyball and table tennis. For those musically inclined, the inn has two recent additions: an 1850 Prince melodeon that has been restored to perfect working order, and a piano on loan from the neighboring Red Fox Music Camp.

The culinary philosophy of the inn, according to managers Bob and Diane Rolfs, is to create meals that are at once "festive and simple—dishes that best set off the essential flavors of fresh and wholesome ingredients." Meals are served family style; and in the morning, Bob and Diane will serve their guests freshly squeezed orange juice and homemade cereal. For later meals, the wine list is quite extensive, especially for an inn of this size. After dinner guests may want to sit on the screened-in porch and treat themselves to a liqueur.

The Sunday brunch is always popular: homemade pecan rolls, chicken livers, baked ham, eggs, pancakes and wonderfully rich coffee.

Be advised to make reservations as early as possible. The inn's reputation is growing, and already many people must be regretfully turned away. The attic accommodations, roomy enough for an entire family,

A quiet spot on the inn's 200 acres.

are so popular that even David Schwarz, the owner, who hails from Larchmont, New York, needs a reservation to get in. The other rooms express a pure New England charm—roomy, with alcoves, exposed beams, braided rugs, patchwork quilts and small sitting rooms. The four-poster mahogany bed in Room 1 is more than 200 years old.

THE FLYING CLOUD INN, Box 143, New Marlboro, Mass. 01230; (413) 229-2113; Bob and Diane Rolfs, Innkeepers. A 1771 farmhouse, with 9 bedrooms, ideally situated in the heart of the Berkshires. Open about May 4 to Oct. 28. Rates from $46 to $50 per person, private bath; $41 to $45 per person, shared bath. Single occupancy surcharge $20. All rates include breakfast, dinner and gratuities. Lunch available at an additional charge. Dining room not open to the public. Children welcome; no pets. No credit cards. Many recreation facilities including tennis (with instruction available), swimming, fishing, bicycling, ping pong, croquet, badminton, board games and an interesting library.

DIRECTIONS: From New York City, take I-684 to 84 East to Conn. 8 North to 44 West to 183 North 14.5 miles to inn. From Boston, take I-90 to Exit 2 (Lee), then 102 to 7 South, to 23 East to 57. Beyond New Marlboro, take right fork off 57, 2 miles to inn.

An 18th-century canopy bed, made of Honduras mahogany.

Gourmet specialties in a transformed barn

Tucked away in Scituate Harbor, a fishing village twenty miles southeast of Boston, the Inn for All Seasons offers a dining experience that deserves to be savored, from the delicious appetizers to the rich desserts, served by the formally attired staff.

As innkeepers, Elaine and Ed Wondolowski set forth their dinner goals: "The entire production, as in a well-performed symphony, must be perfectly balanced, precisely delivered, aesthetically appealing and, above all, delectable." The *Boston Globe* was impressed and ranked the inn's kitchen among the top ten in eastern Massachusetts.

The dining staff seems to anticipate guests' every need. Several of the waiters have been known to memorize orders for tables of six or more and serve each course without error or delay. Memorable dishes of the house include mushrooms Sam Ward, served under glass with toasted croutons; a broiled ham slice with the delectable Sam Ward sauce. Also special are the artichoke hearts stuffed with crab meat, served either hot or cold, and the crab crown Pompadour with chopped truffles, served with fresh asparagus and sautéed cherry tomatoes. The almond peach pie is a delight.

No matter what the season, there is always fresh fish from local waters, and the shrimp and crab Dijon are innovative and delicious.

"Dining is our bright star at the moment," says Elaine, and she is doing everything possible to main-

tain that same high quality in the rest of the inn. A remarkable transformation has taken place, considering that the building was once a barn.

A 1952 Alvis sedan at the front door sets the tone for the imaginative touches within. Each dining room has a special atmosphere, from darkly romantic to sweetly nostalgic, decorated with framed sheet music from another era, including such heady tunes as "Red Rose Rag," "Take Me Back to the Garden of Love" and "In the Shade of the Old Apple Tree."

The foyer is a grand turn-of-the-century parlor with a piano crowned by a large ceramic zebra, one of several striking animals imported from a gift shop Elaine once owned. The seven guest rooms upstairs are all completely different and range from the vivid Red Room, to the Gold Room, with four-poster beds and an Indian rug, and the understated Pine Room, brightened with traditional green ticking. Two of the rooms have porches, and all share baths.

Local attractions include four public beaches, boating and fishing. And for a special treat, food and wine seminars are conducted by Elaine at the inn.

The innkeeper's 1952 Alvis welcomes visitors at the inn's front door.

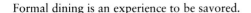

Formal dining is an experience to be savored.

INN FOR ALL SEASONS, 32 Barker Rd., Scituate Harbor, Mass. 02066; (617) 545-6699; Elaine and Ed Wondolowski, Innkeepers. A 7-room inn, with 4-star restaurant, in a fishing village 20 miles from Boston. Shared baths. Open all year. Dining room, open for lunch and dinner except Mondays, features Continental cuisine and fresh local fish. Rates $27 to $34 double, including Continental breakfast. Children welcome; no pets. Visa and Master Charge credit cards accepted. Golf, tennis, swimming and 4 public beaches nearby. Food and wine seminars at inn.

DIRECTIONS: From Boston, take S.E. Expressway South to Route 3 and continue to Norwell-Scituate exit. Turn left off ramp onto Route 53. At first traffic light, turn right on Route 123. Continue to next traffic light, cross intersection into Scituate Harbor. At next traffic light, turn right and at second major turnoff, go left on Barker Rd. to inn.

The peak of perfection in a Nantucket inn

The Jared Coffin House was built in 1845 by a wealthy Nantucket shipowner. It was the first three-story house on the island and built entirely of English brick with a roof of Welsh slate. Houses at that time were usually built of wood, but Coffin wanted something more imposing, befitting his stature, and had the building materials brought across the Atlantic as ballast in his ships.

Through the years, the Jared Coffin House has had a series of owners, not all of whom treated it kindly. But in 1961, it was bought by the Nantucket Historical Trust as part of the restoration plan for the island and painstakingly restored. Now owned and skillfully operated by Philip and Peggy Read, it is one of the finest inns in New England. Everything in the house, from the antique furniture, Oriental rugs and other evidences of the China trade, to the materials for the drapery and upholstery, is in keeping with the period. The guest rooms—most with canopied four-posters— are bright and spacious, and many have fireplaces and baths. The full-service dining room presents an excellent and extensive menu and is one of the few restaurants on the island open all year.

Nantucket, with its fabulous beaches and sailing, is primarily a summer resort, but its charm can be even better appreciated in the off-season, when visitors can quietly and peacefully enjoy the lovely community with its palpable sense of history. The Folger Museum holds a treasury of artifacts and memorabilia of the island's history, much of it donated by Nantucket families. The Whaling Museum, next door, displays everything imaginable related to whaling, even a real whale skeleton, and the life-size re-creations of the various "shops" needed to make each whaling ship self-sufficient are fascinating.

When staying at the Jared Coffin House, guests are treated to the very real feeling of what it was like when Nantucket, with its brick sidewalks and cobblestone streets, was a bustling whaling port.

The Nantucket "islanders" are fiercely proud of their home and don't think there is any other place on

earth really worth worrying about. Visitors come away with the suspicion that they may be right.

JARED COFFIN HOUSE, Broad St., Nantucket Island, Mass. 02554; (617) 228-2400; Philip and Margaret Read, Innkeepers. A 46-room inn in Nantucket's most imposing mansion, dating from 1845, and beautifully restored and furnished in period. Private baths. Open all year. Rates $20 to $30 single; $40 to $55 double. Full service dining room open all year. Visa, Master Charge, American Express and Diners Club credit cards accepted. Confirmed reservations imperative.

DIRECTIONS: Year-round ferry from Woods Hole, Mass. From Hyannis, ferry runs May through Oct. Call (617) 548-5011 for ferry reservations, required to take automobiles to island. Inn is up Broad St., 300 yards from ferry dock. Air service from Hyannis, Boston, New York.

The fully restored 1845 mansion is one of New England's most famous guest houses. *Left*: Two of the guest rooms. OVERLEAF: Private houses line the wharves in Nantucket harbor and the following pages show a cobbled shopping street in the town and bicycles at the beach.

Stay overnight, then buy your bed!

To give some idea of the furnishings at this memorable Cape Cod inn, a quote from owner Jack Schwarz is enlightening. "This inn was decorated 100 percent by my wife in conjunction with *Architectural Digest.*"

That statement should conjure up visions of stately rooms, with elegant touches and artistic design. And those visitors who fall in love with a particular piece are in luck: much of the inn's furniture is for sale, because it doubles as the White Elephant Antique Shop. Rarely do people have a chance to try out antiques before they buy, but at The Nauset House Inn, this is one of the lovely side benefits.

For those who are just looking, there is plenty to see, from the antique Glasgow drum in the white-on-white living room, the porcelain swan from England and the Early American bottle collection, to the turn-of-the-century greenhouse.

Jack was formerly regional manager at a company selling electrical motors and was just about to be transferred to the Midwest when he decided to buy the inn. His wife, Lucille, was an ad agency executive, and both the Schwarzes are former pilots.

Lucille seems to have boundless energy and can be seen darting in and out of the kitchen, taking their spirited boxer Ug (for ugly) out for a stroll or bringing in fresh flowers to brighten a room.

"You get pretty arts and craftsy here during the winter," says Jack, and it doesn't take long to see how imaginations can roam. The Nauset House Inn logo is an Indian called Jacques, who comes complete with his own history. According to local legend, Jacques was the product of a liaison between the Duke of Orleans and an Indian maiden of the Nauset tribe in the bushes where The Nauset House Inn now stands. The Schwarzes have framed Jacques's story, and it is one of the many charming features of the inn.

The breakfast room is filled with authentic Early American pieces. OVERLEAF: the understated inn doubles as an antiques shop.

The living room is a restful white-on-white.

Breakfast, the inn's only meal, is an intimate affair, with two sittings to accommodate guests from the fourteen rooms. The menu changes daily and often features quiche, bacon, hot chocolate, peach or cranberry muffins, eggs and sour-cream coffee cake.

Guest rooms in the three brown clapboard buildings range from ornate to austere, but all are comfortable and eye-catching. For sun worshipers, there is a brick patio out back, and the seashore is just a short walk from the inn's back door.

THE NAUSET HOUSE INN, P.O. Box 446, Beach Rd., East Orleans, Mass. 02643; (617) 255-2195; Jack and Lucille Schwarz, Innkeepers. An elegant, 14-room Cape Cod inn near the ocean. Open from about April 1 to November 15. Rates are $18 single, with shared bath, to $35 for an extra large double room with bath and sitting area. A complete and delicious breakfast, the only meal served, is $3 additional. No children under 12; no pets. Visa and Master Charge credit cards accepted. Tennis, golf, riding, swimming, sailing nearby.

DIRECTIONS: From Route 6 on Cape Cod, take Exit 12 and follow signs to Nauset Beach. Inn is on Nauset Beach Rd., ½ mile before beach.

Traditional feasting, modern comfort

Ebenezer Crafts, who built his store and tavern in 1770, was one of the town's leading citizens—storekeeper, publican, businessman, often the local banker. His busy tavern was by far the best source of news for the local citizenry during the turbulent days leading up to the American Revolution. When word came of the shots fired at Lexington and Concord, Ebenezer formed a company of cavalry from among his customers and went off to war.

Today, the Publick House still dispenses traditional New England hospitality in historic Sturbridge. The hallways and sloping irregular floors, some of them made from red pine now rare in New England, bespeak its eighteenth-century heritage, while the air conditioning, modern baths and telephones in every room make it a very up-to-date facility. The twenty-one guest rooms are well designed and comfortable. With exposed oak beams and many old-fashioned decorative touches, such as the wooden ice bucket that doubles as a waste basket, flowered wallpaper, white organdy curtains and a tall chair with its own writing arm, a room in the Publick House combines the best in traditional and contemporary innkeeping. The public sitting rooms, with beautiful braided rugs and wide plank floors, feature a brace of cozy chairs, perfect for snoozing. The taproom has a huge, walk-in fireplace and a fine collection of copper kettles and pots. The inn's dining room, in the old barn, can accommodate as many as 200 guests; but the old timber stalls break up the room nicely and allow for considerable privacy. The Pumpkin Room, one of the private dining facilities, is named for its mellow pumpkin pine paneling, hung with New England Primitives. Chef Al Cournoyer has eight full-time cooks and five bakers who provide many delicious specialties, and their traditional farmer's breakfast is famous. Guests with hearty appetites stow away hot mulled cider, red flannel hash with eggs, freshly baked breads, muffins, pecan rolls, deep-dish apple pie and pots of coffee.

The Publick House is kept bustling all year; but in the winter, there are several special weekend parties, with horse-drawn sleigh rides. The inn goes all out for Christmas. It keeps the traditional Twelve Days with a riot of celebrations, and the final holiday feast features a Boar's Head Procession, with a roast suckling pig, roast goose, platters of venison and plum pudding.

Old Ebenezer Crafts would be delighted with his tavern today.

Christmas is a time of great celebration, with Yuletide festivities continuing for weeks.

This sitting room has remained almost unchanged for more than 200 years.

PUBLICK HOUSE, on the Common, Sturbridge, Mass. 01566; (617) 347-3313; Buddy Adler, Innkeeper. A 21-room inn in a pre-Revolutionary tavern near Old Sturbridge Village restoration. Private baths. Open all year. Rates during the fall foliage high season from the end of Sept. through Oct. $40 double. Regular season, Nov. through mid-Sept. $35 double. Suites, regular season, $48 to $55; high season, $55 to $65. Breakfast, lunch and dinner served daily in 5 dining rooms. Yankee cooking a specialty. Traditional feasts and festivities during the Twelve Days of Christmas. Children and pets accepted. Visa, Master Charge, American Express and Diners Club credit cards accepted. Lakes nearby; special Yankee winter weekends.

DIRECTIONS: From Hartford, Conn., take I-84. It becomes I-86, then continue to Exit 3, Sturbridge. From Albany or Boston area, take Mass. Turnpike to Exit 9. Inn is on Sturbridge Common, Route 131.

In Ebenezer Craft's day, meals were cooked in this enormous walk-in fireplace, *above*. Private dining facilities include The Pumpkin Room, *left*, so named for its pumpkin pine walls.

Upstairs, the guest rooms feature comfortable beds in a Colonial atmosphere with all of the modern amenities.

A fabled inn in a historic town

Stockbridge has been inexorably woven into the intellectual and social history of New England ever since the brilliant Puritan clergyman Jonathan Edwards first took up his pastoral duties there in 1751. The Red Lion Inn, preaching a somewhat different doctrine, was built in 1773 and became a favorite gathering place for some of New England's brightest literary lights. Emerson and Longfellow were frequent visitors, and when two of America's foremost nineteenth-century authors, Hawthorne and Melville, finally met after years of friendly correspondence, it was here. The inn has been a favorite stopping place for performers at the Berkshire Playhouse since the 1920s, and the famous English character actor Sir C. Aubrey Smith said he never felt more at home in America than when he was staying at the Red Lion. Today, visitors and artists attending Tanglewood and the Jacob's Pillow Dance Festival often stay here.

Saved from demolition to make way for a supermarket by John and Jane Fitzpatrick in 1968, the Red Lion Inn is filled with priceless antiques, many in continuous use for more than a century. The well-organized and comfortably furnished lobby gives the impression of a neat New England living room. Many works by Stockbridge's most famous resident artist, Norman Rockwell, are well displayed. The inn

has more than a hundred rooms, and the upper floors are reached either by a fine Colonial Revival staircase or by a sturdy, turn-of-the-century cage elevator, painted silver and still doing yeoman's work.

The year-round attractions in the Stockbridge area are many, but when the fall foliage attracts too many "leaf-peepers" for the Red Lion Inn and other facilities to handle, the overflow, if they are willing, can find slightly less luxurious accommodations—in the local jail.

A review given to the inn in 1850, when it was the Stockbridge House operated by Mr. and Mrs. Charles Plumb, is as true today as the day it was written: "The Stockbridge House has been put in perfect order from garret to cellar, and with its open fireplaces, its quaint and comfortable furniture, and ancient bric-a-brac, it offers a delightful abode, seldom to be found in a country village."

Corner suite, with Victorian antiques.

Three teapots from the inn's vast collection of antiques, china and pewter. OVERLEAF. *Top left:* part of the building's fascinating facade; *lower left:* gourds decorate the sideboard beneath a German winter landscape in the dining room. *Right:* a porch retreat with a seasonal motif.

THE RED LION INN, Main St., Stockbridge, Mass. 01262; (413) 298-5545; John and Jane Fitzgerald, Owners. Betsy Holtzinger, Innkeeper. A 105-room historic inn in the beautiful southern Berkshires. Private and shared baths; air-conditioned; color TV in some rooms. Open all year. Rates Nov. 1 through June 30, midweek, $24 to $36 double; $18 to $22 single. Suite $54. Weekend, $30 to $36 double; $24 to $28 single. Suite $62. From July 1 through Oct. 31, midweek, $30 to $36 double; $24 to $28 single. Suite $62. Weekend, $40 to $52 double; $34 to $40 single. Suite $92. Extra guest in room $10. Dining room and Widow Bingham Tavern open daily for breakfast, lunch and dinner. In good weather, guests may dine in flower-filled courtyard. Children welcome; pets $7.50. Visa, Master Charge, American Express and Diners Club credit cards accepted. Swimming pool, gift shop. Golf, tennis, skiing and skating nearby.

DIRECTIONS: From New York City, take I-95. At New Haven, Conn., turn left onto I-91. Turn left again onto Mass. Turnpike, drive to Exit 2 and turn left to Stockbridge. Inn on Main St.

A splendid inn, aptly named

Although Orin Flint had a degree in electrical engineering and Martha Flint had a degree in business administration, when they decided to open their own business, they thought their talents would best be combined in innkeeping.

They looked for a long time and finally found a Victorian mansion in Whitinsville that had been built in 1871 for the owner of the local cotton mill. It was basically sound but needed some work, and while Orin took care of the repairs, Martha haunted the flea markets and chose furnishings for the inn that were true to its Victorian heritage.

When The Victorian opened in 1975, it had been completely renovated and modernized. The mansard-roofed house, with its magnificent, Italianate façade, is painted white, and the front doors have panels of etched glass. The high-ceilinged rooms are amply proportioned, and the hammered-copper chandelier in the wide front hall, part of the original furnishings, has already caught the approving and covetous eye of the Museum of Fine Arts in Boston. To the left of the front hall, elegant draperies set off the golden chandelier in a small dining room, formerly a parlor, and the rich blue of the moiré wall covering is repeated in the table linen. Off the hall to the right is the largest of the three dining rooms. Once the library, it runs the full length of the house, and it still contains bookshelves filled with an extensive collection amassed by a former owner on every subject from ecclesiastical history to beekeeping. The tables are resplendent with sparkling glassware and candelabra.

A splendid mahogany staircase leads to the commodious guest rooms upstairs. The former master bedroom has a separate dressing room with mirrored

Magnificent meals in luxurious surroundings.

doors and a tufted, red velvet chaise longue. The baths combine Victorian spaciousness with modern fixtures, while another modern amenity, the air conditioner, has been neatly hidden.

The Flints were right to choose innkeeping as their career. They had an immediate and instinctive grasp of its essential elements: the comfort of their guests and concern for the kitchen. The cuisine is French, and the meals are beautifully presented. Each table has its own loaf of freshly made herb bread, and the rich desserts are a perfect ending for the meal.

The time warp at the Victorian has taken us back a hundred years. And the time is right.

THE VICTORIAN, 583 Linwood Ave., Whitinsville, Mass. 01588; (617) 234-2500; Orin and Martha Flint, Innkeepers. As its name implies, this 7-room inn, midway between Worcester, Mass. and Providence, R.I., is housed in a Victorian mansion authentically furnished in keeping with the period. Private and shared baths. Open all year. Rates from $25 to $50 double, including Continental breakfast. The restaurant offers a fine French menu at lunch, Tuesday through Friday, and dinner daily, except Monday. Children welcome. Pets accepted at innkeepers' discretion. Visa, Master Charge and American Express credit cards accepted.

DIRECTIONS: From north on Route 146, take Purgatory Chasm exit to Whitinsville. Take right at traffic light in town center onto Linwood Ave. Inn is on left about 1 mile beyond center. From south on 146, take Uxbridge exit, proceed about 2 miles beyond U bridge traffic light on Route 121 to sign for Whitinsville. Turn left; inn is on right beyond millpond.

The inn's décor is almost legendary in its perfection, as this sumptuous dressing room in the main guest room shows. OVERLEAF. *Left:* The Victorian's Italianate facade. *Right:* floral patterns abound at the inn, from tiny wildflowers in a basket to daisies outside the greenhouse.

Italian palazzo in the Berkshires

When most Americans think of "a little place in the country," they usually imagine a small vine-covered cottage far from the busy city, with a white picket fence and a bed of petunias near the door. Well, the wealthy and titled need a little place in the country, too, and when the daughter of a rich American industrialist married an Italian count in the 1920s, her father re-created, as their wedding present, a sixteenth-century Florentine palace in the Berkshires. He imported 150 workmen from Italy for the construction and reputedly spent $1 million just to build this dream cottage.

Sold by the countess's heirs in the late 1940s, it was down at the heels by the time David Weisgal bought and restored it in 1976. Fortunately for the old house, both he and Florence Brooks-Dunay had the vision and taste to revive it. David says, "We didn't really look on this as a commercial enterprise. We bought it mainly for a change, a new way of life. I think of it as our home, to which people are invited as guests." Florence took on the redecorating and has complemented the predominantly noble Renaissance touches with bright colors, wicker and crisp, modern fabrics. A profusion of hanging plants add to the comfortable and lived-in atmosphere. The guest rooms are either regular or deluxe; one of the latter is huge, with its own fireplace, two canopied beds and French doors leading to a private terrace looking toward the swimming pool. The Aviary, a duplex suite with its own spiral staircase, is often used by Leonard Bernstein when he is performing at Tanglewood. Some of the comfortable furniture is then removed to make way for his grand piano.

Although relatively inexperienced at innkeeping, Florence, a former dancer, and David, a former fund-raising executive, are doing a splendid job. A jack-of-all-trades, he personally greets guests and sees them settled. He fetches the wood and usually tends the bar in what was once the library. He is a past master at making omelettes, which he sometimes creates for the leisurely breakfasts. The screened-in pergola, just off the main terrace, is a delightful spot for a summer lunch; and the other meals are served in the dining room, cheerfully accented in red, with bentwood chairs and round tables. The cuisine offers both Continental and American specialties, and the chef's homemade pecan pie is delicious.

The lower Berkshires are famous for their cultural events—the Tanglewood and Jacob's Pillow festivals—and all manner of sports are available. But the main attraction for its guests is Wheatleigh itself. Relaxing in this fabulous setting is a fantasy come true.

WHEATLEIGH, P.O. Box 824, Lenox, Mass. 01240; (413) 637-0610; A. David Weisgal and Florence Brooks-Dunay, Innkeepers. An 18-room inn in a romantic Palladian villa near Tanglewood. Private baths. Open all year. Rates, including full breakfast, from $45 to $100 double, depending on season and whether accommodations are for midweek or weekend. Dining room serves breakfast daily, lunch and dinner Wednesday through Sunday during summer season, Friday and Saturday in off-season. Children not encouraged; no pets. Visa, Master Charge and American Express credit cards accepted. Swimming pool, tennis court. Tanglewood Music Festival within walking distance. Inn is available by the day for small executive conferences and seminars.

DIRECTIONS: From New York City, take Taconic Pkwy. to Hillsdale exit. Go east on Route 23 into Route 7 going north to Stockbridge. Drive straight ahead up the hill at junction with Stockbridge main street. Inn entrance on right about 4½ miles. From Lenox, take Old Stockbridge Rd. to Hawthorne; continue to stop sign, turn left 200 yards to inn entrance.

Elaborate Venetian candlesticks rest on a hand-carved mantel in the palazzo's original dining room, where guests are served breakfast and dinner. Wheatleigh's largest guest room overlooks Stockbridge Bowl. OVERLEAF: the south terrace of Wheatleigh, "showplace of the Berkshires."

A country inn with two PhD's

From the exterior, the white clapboard Williamsville Inn resembles a typical New England country inn. Once inside, visitors are in for some surprises. This may be the only country inn run by two certified PhDs, or with a grandmother on the staff who "inn sits"—not to mention the neighbors from the Boston Symphony Orchestra who drop by to use the pool. And last but not least, don't forget the orange and carrot soup.

The food is first rate, and Lenora Bowen, a self-taught chef and co-owner, is the person responsible. A former college math professor, she has become a master of French cooking. *Boston* magazine's restaurant reviewer has ranked the Williamsville Inn cuisine number one in a survey of regional country inns. One food critic has said that it is worth the trip just to sample the soups. And the entrées are equally good: try the chicken with artichokes, mushrooms and Gruyère or the duckling à l'orange made with a Grand Marnier and Madeira sauce.

Up front, Lenora's husband, Stuart, is a gregarious host, greeting the inn's many repeat guests. Stuart earned his PhD as an environmental engineer and decided to chuck his promising career a few years ago because of too much paperwork and not enough people. The Bowens also wanted to try working together, and now the whole family is in the act.

Lenora's mother, who formerly managed a dress shop, handles the books, helps out with breakfast and occasionally "inn sits" when Lenora and Stuart want a few days off. Thirteen-year-old Elise takes care of salads and breads, and fifteen-year-old Scott helps his father around the house.

As for lodgings, the main building, a converted farmhouse, has ten rooms, and there are an extra four out back in what was originally a barn. Guest rooms typically have old beds, some with handsome headboards. Other country touches prevail—braided rugs, old-fashioned washbasins and other such items. All rooms have baths, and some are air conditioned.

The inn is a favorite among Tanglewood devotees in summer; but no matter what the season, there is always something to enjoy, from skiing and antiquing, to hiking and fishing and gazing at Tom Ball Mountain on the other side of the inn.

Old fashioned guest rooms are in two homey settings—the main house and a converted barn. The summer dining porch is just beyond the red door.

Lenora and Stuart Bowen, who both have PhD's, are innkeepers at this lively Berkshire inn.

THE WILLIAMSVILLE INN, Route 41, West Stockbridge, Mass. 01266; (413) 274-6580; Lenora and Stuart Bowen, Innkeepers. A converted Berkshire farmhouse and barn, with 14 charmingly decorated guest rooms. All rooms have private baths; some are air conditioned. Open all year except Wednesdays in summer and fall; Tuesdays and Wednesdays the rest of the year. Closed November 1 to Thanksgiving eve; closed Christmas. Rates $28 to $52 single or double. Breakfast is served to inn guests only at an additional charge. The dining room, featuring a sophisticated Country French cuisine, is open for dinner and lunch on Saturday and Sunday during summer and fall. Children welcome; no pets. Visa and Master Charge credit cards accepted. Swimming and tennis on inn grounds; cross-country skiing nearby.

DIRECTIONS: From New York City, take Sawmill River Pkwy. to Taconic Pkwy., exit at Hillsdale and take Route 23 East through Great Barrington to Route 41 North. Inn is 5 miles north on the left. From Boston, take Mass. Turnpike West to Exit 1. Turn left on Route 41 South and continue 5 miles to inn on right.

Two family inns on a picturesque cape

Back in 1946, war-weary Fred and Lydia Wemyss took their young family to Rockport for a weekend of rest and relaxation. Thirty years and some four inns later, Fred and Lydia and their son Gary are the owners of a thriving country inn business in that historic old town they loved so much. The Yankee Clipper Inn, comprising three converted houses, is run by the senior Wemysses, and the Ralph Waldo Emerson Inn, a huge old white hotel down the street, is the province of their son Gary. Among the sixty rooms at the two inns, there is such a wide variety of accommodations and activities that almost everyone can find something to please.

The prevailing theme is nautical. The Wemysses love the ocean and have gone to great pains to share their affection by providing a seaside resort. Seafood is the mainstay of the menu, and most of the rooms have oceanfront views, including the dining room at the Yankee Clipper, which is completely enclosed by glass. The guest rooms are named after clipper ships, and one, the SOS Room, even has a porthole in the shower.

Hand-turned stairway from the Bullfinch house.

The Yankee Clipper's three main buildings have diverse furnishings from all over the world.

The Inn, a Georgian mansion with dining rooms and a saltwater pool, is the center of activity for the Yankee Clipper complex. Rooms vary in size and furnishings, but most are filled with antiques and offer oceanfront views. The wraparound porches are particularly pleasant for watching the sunrise over the water, and the blue wicker porch of the Red Jacket Room is especially appealing. And for those who like sleigh beds, the SOS Room has two.

Trekking through a flower garden, visitors come to The Quarter Deck, a more contemporary dwelling with seven attractive guest rooms, six with huge picture windows facing the ocean—or more aptly, bordering on the ocean. The water appears to be right outside the window, and the thought of diving in to take a swim is tempting. Fred Wemyss, an intrepid poet, likes to call the view his "landlubber's cruise"—"All of the ocean with none of the motion."

Across the street from these two buildings is the Bullfinch House, an 1840 Greek Revival home that

was named for its renowned architect and is a favorite spot for visiting architects. The rooms are somewhat small, but the decorative lintels, delicate hand-turned stairway, multiple ceiling moldings and numerous other architectural details have a special charm that more than compensates for any limitations in size. Some of the leaded-glass windows are slightly cracked, but Fred refuses to replace anything that might be of historic interest. On one window is a woman's name etched with a diamond ring back in 1863.

Food at the Yankee Clipper Inn is good, down-home fare. "The staff cooks the way I want them to," says Fred, "Fannie Farmer and *Joy of Cooking*." The corn chowder, blueberry pancakes, zucchini bread, mock cheesecake and baked scrod are delicious, as are the cranberry Bavarian mousse and fudge pies. Vegetables are generally fresh, and steamed lobsters are available most nights.

Over at the Ralph Waldo Emerson Inn, named for the great New England author who was a frequent guest, the atmosphere is a skillful blending of the old and new. The four-story white building is reminiscent of a large old hotel, with its high-ceilinged living room, old-fashioned bedrooms and oversized porch. The oldest part of the building, an 1806 tavern, was moved to its present site in 1912, at which time a major section was added. On the contemporary side, the inn boasts a mini-movie theater, along with a sauna and jacuzzi room that can be reserved by the hour.

There is a swimming pool in back and a large open area where you can enjoy the view of the ocean or watch the weekly sailboat races. Guest rooms tend to have a turn-of-the-century look, with globe lamps, glass door transoms and soft pastel curtains. The

The Ralph Waldo Emerson building.

rooms are comfortable and airy, and all have private baths.

Meals are simple, with a daily meat and fish entrée and a special baked stuffed lobster. "People want to know if our lobster is from Maine," says Gary. "Sometimes they think they *are* in Maine. No, sir, I tell them. Everything here is from Rockport Bay."

He can be a bit chauvinistic, but since he has grown up in such a fascinating old town, he probably has a right to be. There is nothing like his inevitable retort to the baffled tourist. "When they want to know where they are, I tell them we're bordered by Gloucester on one side and Portugal on the other."

YANKEE CLIPPER INN, 127 Granite St., Rockport, Mass. 01966; (617) 546-3407; Fred and Lydia Weymss, Innkeepers. A 25-room seaside inn housed in 3 buildings. Private baths. Open all year. Off-season rates (May 14 to July 1; Sept. 4 to Oct. 31) $30 to $40 double, $18 single, without meals. $60 to $66 double, $31 single, with breakfast and lunch. In season (July 1 to Labor Day) $35 double, $22 single, without meals. $70 to $80 double, with breakfast, lunch and dinner. 15% gratuity charge. Dining room open to guests only. Children welcome; no pets. No credit cards accepted. Swimming pool. Golf, sailing, boating nearby.

DIRECTIONS: From New York City, take Mass. Turnpike to exit for Route 128 North. At Gloucester, turn left at first set of traffic lights onto Route 127. Drive 5 miles to large intersection in Rockport, turn left again at sign for Pigeon Cove and Annisquam. Inn is on Route 127 at the ocean.

RALPH WALDO EMERSON INN, Cathedral Ave., Rockport, Mass. 01966; (617) 546-6321; Gary Wemyss, Innkeeper. A 37-room inn, named for the celebrated New England author. Private baths. Open Memorial Day weekend through Oct. 12. Rates in season (July 1 through Labor Day) $28 to $48 double; $20 to $31 single, without meals. $50 to $70 double; $31 to $42 single, with breakfast and dinner. Off-season, $25 to $40 double; $16 to $23 single. Breakfast $3. Crib or cot in room $5. 15% gratuity charge. Swimming pool, sauna, whirlpool.

DIRECTIONS: On Route 127 in Rockport, drive 2 miles beyond Yankee Clipper, turn right at sign for inn and drive to end of street.

Guest room at the Ralph Waldo Emerson.

Rockport is well-known for its ocean views and its fishing—some of the best in the Northeast.
Left: the Yankee Clipper building.

Luxurious "cottage" in fabled Newport

Newport was once described as a place where people who don't have a care in the world go to get away from it all. Ever since the first "cottages" were erected in stone and marble more than a century ago by some of America's wealthiest families, Newport has been a national symbol for the elegant life.

The Inn at Castle Hill has a perfect setting on thirty-two acres not far from Jacqueline Kennedy Onassis's childhood home at Hammersmith Farm. Overlooking Newport Harbor on one side and the Atlantic Ocean on the other, this imposing shingled mansion was built in 1874 by Alexander Agassiz, one of the founders of modern marine biology. Castle Hill was his summer home, and many of the family's original furnishings are still there.

Under the direction of its present innkeeper, Paul McEnroe, the Inn at Castle Hill combines a rich and elegant décor with exacting European-style service and a superb kitchen. Wines from Paul's carefully stocked and extensive cellar complement the magnificent meals, and classic dishes are often prepared in chafing dishes at the table by attentive waiters.

Ione Williams, from the Inn at Sawmill Farm, helped Paul with the interior design, and the welcoming lounge and mirrored living hall have a Victorian atmosphere that is carefully preserved throughout the house. The larger dining room's red-upholstered chairs and red carpeting complement the fine paneling; the smaller, bright Sunset Room is painted white, with French doors leading to a terrace. The paneling in some of the ten upstairs guest rooms is chestnut; others have floral-patterned wallpaper and white woodwork. One has a tufted Victorian settee in an alcove, another is furnished with light and airy wicker.

The Inn at Castle Hill is a natural gathering place for celebrities, and when Grace Kelly was on location in Newport for the musical *High Society,* she stayed in one of the small guest houses at Castle Hill. Novelist Thornton Wilder was a frequent guest, and more recently, Sir Laurence Olivier and the cast of *The Betsy* had a clambake there. Perhaps the most celebrated guest of all, however, was the "ghost" who

Elegant dining is *de rigueur.*

rattled around for a few months, turning on the washing machine in the middle of the night, and then disappeared. The explanation that Paul likes best maintains that it was the spirit of Agassiz's daughter-in-law, the last member of the family to own the house, who was checking to see what was going on in her old home. Content that the place was in excellent hands, she went back to her eternal rest.

THE INN AT CASTLE HILL, Ocean Drive, Newport, R.I. 02840; (401) 849-3800; Paul McEnroe, Innkeeper. A 20-room inn, magnificently situated on Newport Harbor. Private and shared baths. Open all year. Restaurant open from Easter until Jan. 1. Lunch and dinner served daily. Cocktail lounge open weekends all year. Rates, including Continental breakfast, $26.50 to $60 double. Additional person $10. Two-room suite $75. Harbor House units $45. Beach houses with kitchen $235 to $260 per week. Children welcome; no pets. Visa and Master Charge credit cards accepted. Three private beaches; tennis and golf nearby.

DIRECTIONS: From downtown Newport, take Bellevue Ave., which becomes Ten Mile Ocean Drive. Follow it around, watch for inn sign on left. Or take Thames St. to a right onto Ocean Drive, watch for inn sign on right just beyond Coast Guard station.

Evening sunlight dapples the rich furnishings of the lounge and, OVERLEAF, casts a golden glow over the inn and its 32 acres of land which command the entrance to Newport harbor. Following is one of the fabulous guest rooms.

Family hotel on scenic Block Island

Block Island's history is a dramatic one, beginning with the Manissean Indians, who named it Little God's Island, to the staunch early New England settlers—a group of debtors on the run—and the whaling captains and their wives, who rallied for temperance by declaring the island dry.

And then there is the romance of a young couple from the mainland who wanted to buy some property, after a lifelong love affair with the island. The land they selected just happened to include a small white hotel with a majestic view, so Justin and Joan Abrams from Providence enlisted the aid of their teenage children and embarked on a new career—innkeeping. They renamed their hotel The 1661 Inn, in honor of the settling of Block Island, and prayed they'd have the stamina to make it through the summer.

Today, a decade after their trial venture, Justin and Joan Abrams are heading up a tiny Block Island empire. In addition to The 1661 Inn, they and their now-grown children own and run The Manisses, a recently restored Victorian hotel and restaurant nearby, and the Sandwich Shoppe just down the hill.

The 1661 Inn is far enough from the busy center of town to preserve a feeling of tranquillity. Upstairs the guest rooms are bright and airy; and although some of them are small, the space has been cleverly used: in one room, a closet has been transformed into a half-bath.

Seafood is the mainstay of the 1661.

Food at the inn is locally produced and served in the ocean-view dining room. The accent is on simply prepared seafood sometimes given an unexpected touch: baked flounder is stuffed with oysters and walnuts or mussels and clams, for example.

Vegetables are grown in the inn's garden across the street, and the Abramses are quick to point out an advantage of this: during a recent storm that grounded the ferries for days, the inn was the only establishment on the island to have fresh vegetables.

For lovers of art, the inn has one of the best collections of old Block Island prints extant, along with woodcuts by Winslow Homer. Bird watchers can visit the nearby bird sanctuary, and, finally, those who love to explore can rent bicycles and snorkels.

Block Island is a perfect spot for leisurely sightseeing. Almost every dwelling on this hilly and scenic island is blessed with a view of the ocean. And its twenty-five miles of coastline abound with the beauties of nature—ducks, birds, seashells, rocks and other flora and fauna.

Rita Abrams, *left*, assistant manager of inn, handles details with vivaciousness and charm.

This breezy summer inn stands on one of the highest parts of romantic Block Island.

THE 1661 INN, Box 367, Block Island, R.I. 02807; (401) 466-2421; Rita, Joan and Justin Abrams, Innkeepers. A 21-room family-run island inn, with 5-room guest house. Private and shared baths. Inn open from end of May to mid-October; guest house open all year. Rates $21 single; $35 to $43 double, including full breakfast. Guest house winter rate $20, no meals. Inn restaurant serves breakfast and dinner by advance reservation. Children over 6 welcome; no pets. Visa, Master Charge and American Express credit cards accepted. Lawn games; bicycles for rent. Ocean swimming, boating nearby.

DIRECTIONS: Take I-95 to New London, Conn. for island ferry. In summer, ferries also run from Pt. Judith, Providence and Newport, R.I. In winter, from Pt. Judith only. For schedules write Interstate Navigation, Box 482, New London, CT 06320.

A sedate country-club atmosphere, bounded by the ocean.

Three-generation inn where guests are perennial

There is something about the Weekapaug Inn that brings to mind the word *conservative*. After three generations of management by the Buffum family, this pleasant oceanfront spot has become a sort of extended family enclave, where many visitors return each summer for meetings of the clan. These guests have been coming to Weekapaug for years, and they like things the way they have always been.

For those who want something more than a country-club atmosphere, the fifty-room inn and cottage complex has a great deal to offer. Activities at Weekapaug include bocce, bridge and bingo, sailing, swimming, tennis and beachcombing along the magnificent Rhode Island beaches.

The inn's three large living rooms are popular areas for meeting old friends and catching up on the winners of last year's bocce tournament, who have all been accorded a place of honor in the inn's scrapbook or on plaques in the front hall. "Never quit Whit" seems to be a perennially favorite contender.

As for the accommodations, the guest rooms are comfortable and modern. The American-plan menu is well balanced, and fresh seafood is a major feature, with broiled lobster a once-a-week entrée. New England squash pie, apple fritters and almond macaroons are some of the inn's popular desserts.

The Weekapaug Inn was originally built in 1899 by Frederick C. Buffum and was the center of the tiny Weekapaug community for many years, until the disastrous hurricane of 1938, when two thirty-foot tidal waves swept half the inn into the sea. Frederick C. Buffum, Jr., son of the original owner, offered a poetic postmortem when he said, "The ocean was not to be denied."

Fortunately, local banks rallied to the cause, and today Robert C. Buffum, grandson of the original founder, and his wife, Sydney, are at the helm of the rebuilt three-story, brown-shingled inn. In the winter, the Buffums move south to Florida to manage the other family inn, the Manasota on the Gulf of Mexico.

WEEKAPAUG INN, Weekapaug, R. I. 02891; (401) 322-0301; Mr. and Mrs. Robert C. Buffum, Innkeepers. A 50-room inn on the ocean that's popular with families who return year after year. Private baths. Open approximately June 20 to Labor Day. Rates $60 to $65 per person, double; $70 to $80 single, including 3 meals a day. Cottages with cooking facilities available at $70 for 2 people. Restaurant open to the public by reservation only. Children welcome; no pets. No credit cards accepted. The many activities include tennis, swimming, sailing, rowing, English croquet and bocce bowling.

DIRECTIONS: From New York City, take I-95 to Route 2 to Route 78 Bypass onto Route 1. Turn left on Route 1 to Dunn's Corners, then right to the shore.

Left and above: the inn's large sitting room offers music, chess, and many other diversions. OVERLEAF: the inn is adjacent to a yacht club and the town beach.

New Preston, Conn. 06777; (203) 868-7918; Jim and Carolyn Woollen, Innkeepers. A 15-room inn on Lake Waramaug. Private baths. Open all year. Rates, single $36–$46 per day; double $31–$38.50 per day, including 3 meals. With breakfast and dinner only, $4 less. Without meals, single $23–$38; double $33–$42. Children welcome; pets accepted. Visa, Master Charge and Diners Club. Swimming, fishing, boating and other water sports on the attractive lake. In winter, it's a popular spot for skiers. There's a ski touring center nearby where equipment can be rented. Beginning cross-country skiers can practice on the snow-covered lake before tackling the trails. Downhill skiing nearby.

DIRECTIONS: From Danbury, Conn., take U.S. Rte. 7 North to New Milford. Take Rte. 202 North to intersection of Rte. 45. Go 1½ miles north on Rte. 45 to inn on right-hand side.

LILO RAYMOND

Litchfield,
Connecticut

MEETINGHOUSE INN

LILO RAYMOND

West St., Litchfield, Conn. 06759; (203) 567-8744; Raymond and Pamela Sass, Innkeepers. A former Colonial home dating from 1760, converted to an inn in 1940. Furnished with many antiques, it combines Colonial ambiance with modern comfort. Nine guest rooms, 1 2-bedroom suite, with private baths and fireplaces. Open all year. Rates, $35–$75 single; $40 double, include complimentary breakfast. Dining room open for lunch and dinner. Facilities for country weddings and private parties; bar lounge with entertainment Thursday–Saturday. Children and pets welcome. Visa, Master Charge and Diners Club. Lakes and recreational facilities nearby.

DIRECTIONS: From I-684, turn east onto I-84 to Waterbury; north on Rte. 8 to Litchfield exit onto Rte. 118. Follow to Litchfield Centre, continue west on Rte. 202 about ¼ mile to inn.

Old Lyme,
Connecticut

OLD LYME INN

85 Lyme St., Old Lyme, Conn. 06371; (203) 434-2600; Kenneth and Diana Milne, Innkeepers. A restored Empire mansion on the main street in Old Lyme's Historic District. Five guest rooms with private baths. Open all year except Mondays. Rates, $27 single; $30 double, include Continental breakfast. The three-star French restaurant serves lunch and dinner, and the cocktail lounge features a beautiful Victorian bar. Children and pets are welcome. Visa, Master Charge and American Express. The inn is convenient to many of Connecticut's famous attractions; there are tennis courts nearby and swimming at the town beaches.

DIRECTIONS: From I-95 going north, take Exit 70 and turn left off ramp. Going south, turn right. Turn right at first traffic light, continue to next light where inn is on the left.

LILO RAYMOND

OLD RIVERTON INN

Riverton, Conn. 06065; (203) 379-8678; Mr. and Mrs. James P. Zucco, Innkeepers. A sophisticated inn that's been dispensing hospitality since 1796, when it was a stagecoach stop. Ten rooms with private baths and air conditioning. Open all year. Rates $11–12.50 per person, including complete breakfast. Generous drinks in Hobby Horse Bar before lunch and dinner in formal Colonial Dining Room or unusual bay-windowed terrace room, with old grindstones set into the floor. Wednesday candlelight buffet. Dining rooms closed Mondays, Tuesdays and month of Jan. Children welcome; pets permitted. Visa, Master Charge and American Express. Fishing and white-water canoeing in river across road. Visits to Hitchcock Chair Factory, Store and Museum and Seth Thomas Clock Factory outlet. Many antique and craft shops nearby. Cross-country and downhill skiing in area.

DIRECTIONS: From Rte. 8, turn off on Rte. 20 just north of Winsted.

SUSAN CRAGIN

RAGAMONT INN

Salisbury, Connecticut

LILO RAYMOND

Main St., Salisbury, Conn. 06068; (203) 435-2372; Rolf and Barbara Schenkel, Innkeepers. This former lovely colonial home in the delightful town of Salisbury is now a popular inn with 14 guest rooms. Private and shared baths. Open from May 1– Nov. 1. Breakfast served to guests only. Lunch and dinner served daily except Mondays. There are two fine dining rooms or, if guests prefer, they may dine outdoors in good weather. Rates $12–$25 single; $22–$36 double. Children and pets welcome. No credit cards. Swimming, boating, tennis and golf are all available nearby.

DIRECTIONS: From the Taconic State Pkwy., go east on Rte. 44 through Amenia and Millerton, N.Y., through Lakeville, Conn. to Salisbury.

WAKE ROBIN INN

Lakeville, Connecticut

Lakeville, Conn. 06039; (203) 435-2515; Tor Olsen, Innkeeper. Considered by many to be the most beautiful inn in America, Wake Robin dates from 1898 and has recently been completely restored. There are 40 rooms with private baths and the inn is open from May 1 through Oct. 31. A Continental breakfast is served to guests only. Restaurant open to the public for dinner. Rates, both single and double, $36–$70. Children welcome; pets permitted in the inn's cottages. Visa and Master Charge. The inn is situated in 15 private acres, with swimming, tennis, golf, riding and boating in the immediate area. The famous Hotchkiss School is nearby.

DIRECTIONS: From New York City, take either Rte. 22 to Amenia, N.Y. and continue on Rte. 44 to Lakeville, or take the Taconic State Pkwy. and turn east onto Rte. 44.

LILO RAYMOND

WHITE HART INN

Salisbury, Connecticut

Village Green, Salisbury, Conn. 06068; (203) 435-2511; John Harney, Innkeeper. "We're as New England as Mom's apple pie," says innkeeper Harney about this big rambling inn with many fireplaces and 20 comfortable guest rooms, with private baths and phones. Special rooms and ramp to dining room for handicapped guests. Open all year. Three meals a day, featuring American, Chinese and French cuisine, served in air-conditioned dining room, patio or screened porch. Colonial Tap Room. Single $20–$32; double $22.50–$38. Children welcome; pets allowed. Visa credit card. Fascinating Country Store sells many old-fashioned goodies including home-baked goods. Golf, tennis, swimming, hiking and skiing nearby.

DIRECTIONS: From I-684, go north to Millerton, N.Y., then east on U.S. Rte. 44 to inn at junction of Rte. 41 in Salisbury.

LILO RAYMOND

BLANTYRE CASTLE

Lenox, Massachusetts

GEORGE W. GARDNER

Opposite, one of the castle's magnificent public rooms.

P.O. Box 717, Lenox, Mass. 01240; (413) 637-0475; Jim and Madeline Donahue, Innkeepers. Built in 1902 by William Patterson as an anniversary gift to his wife, Blantyre is an exact replica of a castle in Blantyre, Scotland. This romantic inn has 14 guest rooms, with shared baths, in the castle itself. The 14 rooms in the Carriage House and 5 in motel-type accommodations have private baths. All guest rooms are air conditioned. Open all year. Rates, $34–$54 per person, weekends; $28–$43 per person, weekdays, include breakfast and dinner. Restaurant serves breakfast and dinner daily; lunch weekends only. The Below Stairs bar in the castle basement is a quaint copy of a Scottish pub, with dancing to records. Children welcome; no pets. No credit cards. The 85-acre grounds are surrounded by a golf course. Swimming pool and tennis courts.

DIRECTIONS: From Mass. Tpke. I-90, turn off at Lee onto Rte. 7 North. Inn is 10 minutes drive north on Rte. 7. From New York City, take Rte. 7.

CANDLELIGHT INN

Lenox, Massachusetts

52 Walker St., Lenox, Mass. 01240; (413) 637-1555; James DeMayo, Innkeeper. The attractive décor, antique furnishings and profusion of flowers in the rooms and surrounding gardens make this an unusually pleasing hostelry. Winter holidays feature unique seasonal decorations. Six guest rooms with private baths. Open all year. Single $35; double $48 weekly, July and August. Off-season $35–$40. Cocktail lounge and dining room serving gourmet food, highly rated in area, at lunch and dinner. In summer, meals may be enjoyed on the veranda. Children welcome; no pets. Visa, Master Charge and American Express. Tennis courts, ski resorts nearby. Tanglewood Music Festival 4 miles. Summer theater.

DIRECTIONS: From I-684, turn east onto I-84 to Rte. 7 and continue north to Lenox. Inn just off main street.

SUSAN CRAGIN

Jones Rd. at Gifford St., Falmouth, Mass. 02541; (617) 548-2300. The nucleus of this traditional Cape Cod inn is a 1796 red clapboard house and barn on the edge of Jones Pond. Twenty-three guest rooms with private baths. The cottage rooms are especially popular with families. The inn grounds are beautiful year round, and the Coonamessett Inn is especially attractive for an off-season vacation. Open all year. June 18–Sept. 23, double $20–$43. Off-season, single $10–$16; double $20–$23. Three meals are served daily in the luxurious dining room and intimate bar lounge. The menu is large and varied and the food superb. All the attractions of Cape Cod are nearby, including ocean beaches, indoor tennis, squash, racquet ball and golf courses.

DIRECTIONS: Take Rte. 28 at the bridge over the Cape Cod Canal into Falmouth. Turn left on Jones Rd. to intersection of Gifford St.

BERT BIGELOW

Great Barrington, Massachusetts

ELLING'S GUEST HOUSE

SUSAN CRAGIN

R.D. 3, Box 6, 250 Maple Ave., Great Barrington, Mass. 01230; (413) 528-4103; Jo and Ray Elling, Innkeepers. A few years ago, the Ellings abandoned New York City and turned a 1746 Colonial mansion, the Stephen King House, into a comfortable inn. The interior reflects the house's Colonial beginnings; there's a pleasant living room with fireplace, and a porch with magnificent mountain views. The 6 guest rooms have shared and private baths. Open all year. Rates, $14–$20 single; $22–$30 double, in season (July, Aug., holidays). Off-season (April, May, Nov.) all rates $5 less. Rates include breakfast, the only meal served, but being close to the cultural activities in and around the Stockbridge area, there are many fine restaurants nearby. Unusual tree swing, horseshoe pitch, badminton court. Lake or river swimming.

DIRECTIONS: From New York City, take Taconic State Pkwy. North. Turn east on Rte. 23 through Hillsdale, N.Y., to Great Barrington. Or take Rte. 7 all the way.

Great Barrington, Massachusetts

FAIRFIELD INN

Rte. 23, So. Egremont Rd., Great Barrington, Mass. 01230; (613) 528-2720; James Randolph and Trudy Cushner, Innkeepers. An intimate inn, luxuriously furnished with fine antiques, in the midst of Berkshire activities. Twelve spacious guest rooms with baths and air conditioning. Open all year except Tuesdays. Rates, double, $35 Sun. through Thurs. $35–$40 Fri. and Sat. Dining room serves breakfast, lunch and dinner, with emphasis on both Continental and American cuisine. Reservations requested. Children welcome; no pets. Visa and Master Charge. Swimming pool. Tennis, riding nearby. Golf at any of the 14 courses within 20 mile radius, including 1 adjoining inn. Tanglewood Music Festival and Jacob's Pillow within easy driving distance.

DIRECTIONS: From Great Barrington, on U.S. Rte. 7, go west 3 miles on Rte. 23 to inn.

SUSAN CRAGIN

71 Walker St., Lenox, Mass. 01240; (413) 637-2532; Gerhard and Lilliane Schmid, Innkeepers. Internationally renowned as a medal-winning chef, Gerhard Schmid is a master of epicurean specialties. The Schmid's inn is as justly famous for its superb food as for its luxurious accommodations. The 8 large double rooms and 1 suite have private baths; rates vary with the season. $32–$75 double; $64–$130 for suites, including Continental breakfast. Open all year. Restaurant closed for a month in spring and Sept. Children over 8 welcome; no pets. Visa and Master Charge. Dinner served every night in July and Aug.; Wed. through Sun., Sept. through June. Tennis, Tanglewood Music Festival, major ski areas nearby. Cooking school Oct.– May.

DIRECTIONS: From U.S. Rte. 1, turn off onto Rte. 183 and continue north to Lenox. Inn is in center of town.

SUSAN CRAGIN

GEORGE W. GARDNER

Sweet Seasons, the Inn, Box 364, E. Main St., Wellfleet, Mass. 02667; (617) 349-9333; Robert Merrill, Judith Pihl and Anne Fortier, Innkeepers. The management is new and the name may be changed but not the inn's attractiveness nor the excellence of its restaurant. Of 20 guest rooms, all but 2 have private baths. Open mid-May to mid-Oct. Rates $24–$41 double. Suites (5–6 persons) $43–$55. The inn's restaurant, Sweet Seasons, overlooks a rush-bordered pond and serves a family gourmet brunch and dinner daily. Fine cocktails and entertainment for dancing and listening in the Tavern. Children and pets welcome. Visa credit card. Ocean beaches, all popular sports nearby.

DIRECTIONS: Take Rte. 6, the mid-Cape Hwy., to Wellfleet. Turn left at Wellfleet Center sign and continue to inn on right.

Main St., Harwich Port, Mass. 02646; (617) 432-0171; Mrs. Gladys Smith and C. Philip Smith, Innkeepers. A large cheerful inn on a tree-shaded street in a small Cape Cod town. The 90 rooms have private and shared baths, and the inn is open from Memorial Day through mid-Oct. Rates $30–$44 double; $12 single, without meals. With 3 meals, add $20. With breakfast and dinner only, add $14.50. Dining room serves 3 hearty meals, with clam chowder a delectable daily specialty. Children welcome; small, well-behaved pets allowed. Visa, Master Charge and American Express cards accepted in dining room only. Attractive TV viewing room; swimming pool; private beach nearby.

DIRECTIONS: From U.S. Rte. 6, main Mid-Cape Highway, turn right on Rte. 28 and continue to inn in Harwich Port.

LILO RAYMOND

OLD YARMOUTH INN

Rte. 6A, Yarmouth Port, Mass. 02675; (617) 362-3191; Shane E. Peros, Innkeeper. The oldest inn on Cape Cod, the Old Yarmouth maintains its antique charm. Quaint paper hatboxes, old leather suitcases and ancient horse brasses contribute to the atmosphere of yesteryear. Twelve rooms with private baths. Open all year except Christmas. Rates, $20–$40 double, include Continental breakfast. Lunch and dinner served by reservation; seafood is a specialty. Vegetables and salad makings are fresh from the inn's own garden; all pastries are homemade. Children welcome; no pets. Visa and Master Charge. Beaches. Cape Playhouse and Melody Tent theaters nearby.

DIRECTIONS: From U.S. Rte. 6 take Exit 7 to Yarmouth Port and turn right on Rte. 6A. Inn is ½ mile on right.

BERT BIGELOW

VILLAGE INN

SUSAN CRAGIN

Church St., Lenox, Mass. 01240; (413) 637-0020; Richard and Marie Judd, Innkeepers. Landmark inn in a historic town. Twenty-five guest rooms with private and shared baths. Open all year. Rates, double, Nov. through April $20–$30; May, June and major holidays $25–$35; July and Aug. $30–$55; Sept. and Oct. $30–$45. During July–Aug., minimum stay 3 nights. Holiday and fall foliage weekends, minimum stay 2 nights. Attractive lounges with fireplaces. Cocktails, draft beer, wine and light snacks in quaint pub, Poor Richard's Tavern. Dining room serves breakfast and lunch. Children welcome; no pets. No credit cards. Golf, tennis, swimming, riding, hiking and skiing. Tanglewood Music Festival, Jacob's Pillow, summer theaters nearby.

DIRECTIONS: From Rte. 7, exit onto 7A to Lenox. Inn in center of town.

LARCHWOOD INN

176 Main St., Wakefield, R.I. 02879; (401) 783-5454; Francis J. Browning, Innkeeper. A former mansion, set in handsomely landscaped grounds, the Larchwood has 12 guest rooms, with private and shared baths. Open all year. Rates $14–$32. The restaurant, under the supervision of innkeeper-chef Francis Browning, has a deservedly fine reputation. Three meals are served daily in a number of dining rooms. The Crest Room is decorated with shields and tartans of different Scottish clans, intertwined with thistles; the elegant South County Room has murals depicting Rhode Island's regional history. Children and pets welcome. Visa, Master Charge, American Express and Diners Club. Three miles from superb beaches; tennis, bicycling, cross-country skiing nearby.

DIRECTIONS: From I-95, take U.S. Rte. 1 to Pond St. exit. Go left ½ mile to inn.

GEORGE W. GARDNER